What Should I Say?

The Right (and Wrong!) Words and Deeds for
Life's Sticky, Tricky, Uncomfortable Situations

By Shelly Burke, RN

*"A man finds joy in giving an apt reply,
and how good is a timely word!"*
Proverbs 15:23

Copyright © 2007 by Shelly Burke, RN

What Should I Say?
The Right (and Wrong!)
Words and Deeds for Life's Sticky, Tricky,
Uncomfortable Situations
by Shelly Burke, RN

Printed in the United States of America

ISBN 978-1-60266-682-5

All rights reserved solely by the author. The author guarantees all contents are original and do not infringe upon the legal rights of any other person or work. No part of this book may be reproduced in any form without the permission of the author. The views expressed in this book are not necessarily those of the publisher.

Unless otherwise indicated, Bible quotations are taken from the New International Version Study Bible of the Bible, Copyright © 2002 by Zondervan.

Shelmar Publications
42887 G. G. Road
Genoa, NE 68640
(402) 993-2217
shelly@shellyburke.net
www.shellyburke.net

Copyright Dec. 2007

www.xulonpress.com

What People Are Saying

What Should I Say? The Right (and Wrong!) Words and Deeds for Life's Sticky, Tricky, Uncomfortable Situations is a wonderful resource for those needing guidance on being there for friends and loved ones going through life-changing experiences. Shelly Burke has packed wisdom, compassion, and comfort into the pages of this invaluable book.

Carmen Leal, author of *The Twenty-Third Psalm for Caregivers* and *The Twenty-Third Psalm for Those Who Grieve*

Finally! Someone who has been willing to acknowledge those of us who do not fit into the 'norm' of society. We are the childless and infertile of the world who wanted to have children, but could not. Thank you, Shelly, for including scenarios of our misunderstood life's situations in your book!

Diane Black, Co-founder www.childlessnotbychoice.com

What can you say when a loved one of somebody you know dies suddenly and unexpectedly? This book will give you the words and wisdom for what to say and do when nothing you can think of seems right. Shelly has tackled the toughest circumstances we know, and come up with wonderful words to help you get through the awful, awkward silence that stretches before you when confronted with difficult circumstances.

Her insight and compassion show through on every page.

If you've ever found yourself tongue-tied—or with your foot in your mouth all the way up to your knee—this is the book for you. Maybe there is no 'right' thing to say—but this book will help you from saying the wrong things and making the situation worse.

Joy Dannelly, RN

Shelly Burke has done it again, this time with her insightful wisdom aimed at conveying diplomacy and discretion when you find yourself fumbling for what to say. In a book that you'll reference again, Shelly's sensibility shines through, just as it did in *Home is Where the Mom Is*.

You'll want this unique reference at your fingertips when you're at a loss for words, because Shelly's perceptive and sincere advice will serve you well. This book tackles life's ticklish problems in a way no other book has. It picks up where Miss Manners leaves off, by addressing the words to convey a tactful message and counters with what *not* to say as well.

Beth Burke, unrelated freelance editor

In a world where it's easy to remain insulated in our cars, our homes, within our own choice of music and thoughts, day-to-day verbal interaction with others – particularly in times of stress or crisis – is more important than ever. Alas, it's at those very times when most of us "choke" on our thoughts or fall short on courage to engage others in a meaningful, helpful way.

Burke's chapter on Encouraging Words, forged from experience, observation and prayerful consideration is a common-sense approach to what I fear is becoming a lost art – investing one's self in the lives of others. This chapter is a very appropriate "how to" launching point for one wishing to be a friend in times of joy, sorrow and dilemma. If the Biblical Book of Proverbs needed a checklist on caring communications, Shelly Burke has provided it.

Dan M. Crummett, Editor, Rural Life Magazine
www.rurallifemagazine.com

Words and actions have the power to heal or hurt. This well-organized and much-needed guide will give you ideas of how to respond to the difficult situations and people in your life. Learn what to say and do as well as what not to say and do!

Sue Johnson, author *Grandloving: Making Memories with Your Grandchildren,* www.grandloving.com

----

We all have experienced those awkward predicaments of life. Someone is standing in front of us, an emotional wreck..... awaiting our response. Our minds are racing, our palms are sweating. We open our mouths to speak and realize we have no idea what to say! Finally, a guide through life's most awkward and uncomfortable moments. Shelly gives practical advise how to confront your fears, head on, through Christ's compassionate love.

Martha Whited, RN

"What Should I Say?" is a priceless guide for anyone involved in the life of a child with a disability. This highly informative book offers plenty of advice on how best to talk to a disabled or seriously ill child, or the parent of that child, with compassion and understanding. This is an important book for the general public, as well as those who love, live with and care for a disabled child or teenager. Burke should be commended for bringing a sensitive subject to the forefront of public awareness.

Marie D. Jones, Author and mom of a child with cerebral palsy

----

'What Should I Say?' should be on the bookshelf of everyone who has ever been at a loss for words. With this book, you'll never worry about facing a difficult person, or uncomfortable situation again— you'll know exactly what to say and do, and just as importantly, what not to say or do, to make your point. I could have avoided many uncomfortable silences if I'd known what to say to difficult people we all deal with at one time or another .

Rebecca Edwards

Why I Wrote This Book

I never planned to write this book. Then several years ago, in the course of a few weeks, one friend's marriage suddenly and traumatically ended, and another friend's husband was killed in a tragic farm accident.

During the difficult weeks and months following these events, my friends told me several times of things people had said and done that comforted them . . . and things that had been said and done that just added to their pain. Other friends, family members, and acquaintances came up to me during this time, saying they just did not know what to say or do to comfort these women and their children, who had lost so much.

Then my father-in-law was critically injured in a fall, and during his hospitalization and recovery he and my mother-in-law and husband and I experienced many helpful and comforting words and deeds, and some that were not so helpful or comforting.

Around that time I began to notice, in everyday events, and through Bible study, the power of words and their ability to heal, and hurt. In everyday conversations, people began to tell me about various situations they'd been in and how words from others had hurt, or healed.

They shared with me their feelings of helplessness when they did not know what to say when someone was in the midst of a crisis. Sometimes they compensated for their discomfort by saying something—*anything*. Many times, unfortunately, in their haste to fill the silence they said the wrong thing. Other times people dealt with their discomfort by avoiding the person who was suffering. One lady told me how painful it was when, after the death of her baby, she knew people were avoiding her; she would see them in the grocery store, obviously turning away from her because they didn't want to have to talk to her. From my conversations with many people, I suspect they were avoiding her because of their fear of not knowing what to say to someone who had experienced such a devastating loss.

One day I looked back at all of these events—my friends' tough times, my own experiences, what other people told me, what was revealed to me through Bible study—and I knew God was leading me to write this book.

As I told people about my book, they shared more and more events in their own lives, in which words and deeds had helped, and hurt. It seemed I added another section to the book almost daily!

I have several goals in writing *What Should I Say?* Perhaps the most important is to prevent others who are going through a traumatic time from experiencing the pain that my friends sometimes did, by providing an easy-to-use guide to what to say and do when someone is experiencing a great loss.

For the person trying to come up with the right words, it's easy to put foot-in-mouth (or, in some cases, whole-leg-in-mouth!) when talking with someone about any number of tricky, sticky, uncomfortable situations. Therefore, I've included a wide variety of situations you're likely to face at some time (maybe many times), and the words you can say to help—along with the words that will definitely not help.

My prayer is that readers of *What Should I Say? The Right (and Wrong!) Words and Deeds for Life's Sticky, Tricky, and Uncomfortable Situations,* will enable readers to confidently face sticky, tricky, uncomfortable situations, knowing they'll be able to offer the comfort, support, and encouragement someone needs.

Read This First!
How to Use this Book

You probably picked up this book because at one time or another, you've been in a sticky, tricky, or uncomfortable situation in which you just did not know what to say. Maybe you said something—the first thing that came to mind—to avoid an uncomfortable silence or get away from someone who was crying or upset. Maybe you avoided the person altogether because you were at a loss for words. Either way, you probably did not feel good about how you handled it. Look through the pages of this book for that situation; hopefully you'll find you said (and did) the right thing—but if not, you'll know what to say and do the next time you find yourself in those circumstances.

If you're not facing a particular predicament right now, just page through the book to find out what to say in various situations— you're likely to face one or more of the scenarios presented here, perhaps very soon. After reading what to say and do (and not say or do!) you'll be able to confidently face that situation.

The situations presented in this book apply to men and women; for smoother reading I've used "he" and "she" (rather than the more awkward "he/she") alternately, when the comment could apply to either sex. In any of the situations discussed, the person involved could be a "friend," "relative," "neighbor," or an "acquaintance," so those terms, too, are used interchangeably throughout the book.

Suggestions in the *"What to Say," "What Not to Say," "What to Do,"* and *"Don't . . . "* sections range from what you might say to or do for a close friend or relative, to what's appropriate for a casual acquaintance. Use the response that's right for you, depending on your relationship with the person.

Regardless of your relationship with the person, and the circumstances, do not use a response if it is obviously not true in that situation. It's not the 'right' thing to say if it's not true! Instead, choose a variation of one of the responses given, or another response that is true.

Most of the responses and suggestions in the *"What to Say"* and *"What Not to Say,"* as well as *"What to Do,"* and *"Don't . . . "* sections are appropriate in any situation. However, there are exceptions to every rule. On rare occasions a *"Do"* could become a *"Don't"* and vice versa. Personalize what you say and do according to the situation you are in.

Because my faith is a big part of my life, I often make faith-based comments, usually in the context of comforting or reassuring someone. I've found that people of faith might need a reminder of God's love during a hard time, and a person who does not have an active faith might be ready to hear more about God during a time of crisis. Most people find comfort in being reassured that they are in someone's prayers, even if their faith is not strong or active.

Do not make references to God being in control, prayer, heaven, and so on, if you do not truly believe what you are saying. And don't say these things if you know or strongly suspect the comment will offend the person you are talking to (of course you can still pray for a person, even if he or she does not believe in God or prayer). If you are confident a faith statement is appropriate in your situation, adjust it as your religious traditions (Lutheran, Episcopalian, Catholic, Baptist, etc.) and beliefs dictate.

What Should I Say? The Right (and Wrong) Words and Deeds for Life's Sticky, Tricky, Uncomfortable Situations

Brief Table of Contents

Why I Wrote This Book ix
Read This First! How to Use This Book xi

Chapter One: Everyday Situations 21
Chapter Two: Love, Marriage, and Children 53
Chapter Three: Difficult People 81
Chapter Four: Family 99
Chapter Five: Death 119
Chapter Six: Illness and Injury 155
Chapter Seven: Various Sticky, Tricky Situations 177
Chapter Eight: Encouraging Words 215

Acknowledgements 217

Appendix 217
   Asking the Holy Spirit to Guide Your Words 217
   Tone of Voice (Using Tone of Voice to Your Advantage) 218
   10 Worst Things to Say in Any Situation 219
   10 Best Things to Say When You Don't Know What
      to Say 220

Index 221

What Should I Say? The Right (and Wrong) Words and Deeds for Life's Sticky, Tricky, Uncomfortable Situations

Detailed Table of Contents

Why I Wrote This Book	ix
Read This First! How to Use This Book	xi
Chapter One: Everyday Situations	**21**
Advice	21
When Someone Asks for Your Advice	21
Giving Unasked for Advice	22
Asking for Advice	24
If You Receive Unasked for Advice	25
Favors	26
Offering a Favor	26
How to say "No;" Turning Down a Request for a Favor	27
Asking for a Favor	29
Accepting a Favor	31
Turning Down a Favor You're Offered	31
Personal Beliefs and Lifestyle Choices	33
Expressing Yours	33
Others' Lifestyles	34
Religion and Politics	36
If Someone Insults Something Important to You	39
Gossip	40
Should You Tell Someone She's Being Gossiped About?	41
Losing a Job	43
When Someone Loses His Job	43
If You've Lost Your Job	44

Money Problems 45
   *Offering Help to Someone Who is Having Money
      Problems* 45
   If You are Having Money Problems 48
Spouse Bashing...49
Sexist/Racist/Bigoted Remarks or Jokes 50
Uncomfortable Events and When You are Shy......................51

Chapter Two: Love, Marriage, and Children 53
Expressing Concern about a Spouse/Potential Spouse 53
Marriage Problems and Divorce 56
   When Someone is Having Marriage Problems 56
   When Friends Divorce 58
   *Holidays and Wedding Anniversaries During Marriage
      Problems or After Divorce* 59
   *If Your Marriage is in Trouble or You are Getting
      a Divorce*..60
Fertility Problems...61
   When Someone is Having Problems 61
   Announcing a Pregnancy, or Baby Shower 64
   If You are Having Fertility Problems 66
   *If You are Having Fertility Problems and Someone Else
      Becomes Pregnant*..67
Adoption 69
   When Friends Choose to Adopt 69
   If Adoption Plans Fall Through 70
   When You've Adopted 71
Parents and Their Children 72
   Other Children and Your Child..72
   Following Your House Rules..73
   If a Child Won't Follow the Rules 74
   *If You are Uncomfortable with the Environment of Your
      Child's Friend's Home* 75
Kids Behaving Badly 77
If Someone's Kids are Behaving Badly 77
If Someone Else's Kids are Having Problems 78
If Your Kid is in Trouble 80

Chapter Three: Difficult People **81**
   Inappropriate, Rude, Critical, or Obnoxious Questions or
      Comments 81
   The Person Who Talks and Talks and Talks and Talks 83
   The Drama Queen or King 84
   A Person Who is Negative About Everything 86
   If Someone is Always Critical of Others 87
   The Person with a "Poor Me" Attitude 88
   The Person Who Curses in Public 90
   Someone Who is Always Experiencing a Crisis 91
   When Someone Won't Take Responsibility for His or Her
      Problems 93
   Getting Along with Someone Whose Company You do not
      Enjoy 95

Chapter Four: Family **99**
   Your Own Family 100
      General Guidelines for Dealing with Dysfunctional Family
         Members *101*
      If You Don't Want to Stay at a Family Member's
         Home *103*
      If You Don't Want Family Members to Stay at Your
         Home *104*
      Limiting Contact or Cutting off Ties with a Family
         Member *105*
      Explaining Your Actions to Other Family Members *107*
      The Embarrassing Family Member *109*
      If Someone Makes Sexual Comments or Advances *110*
   Your Spouse's Family 111
   A Friend's Family 111
      When a Friend is Having Family Difficulties *111*
      When a Friend Cuts Ties, or Limits Contact with, Family
         Members *113*
      When a Friend's Relative Needs More Care *115*
      When Someone's Relative is in a Long-Term Care Unit *116*

Chapter Five: Death **119**

When a Loved One has Died 119
   In the First Hours and Days After a Loved One
     has Died *119*
   The Days Between the Death and the Funeral *123*
   At the Funeral *125*
   In the Weeks and Months After the Death *126*
   When You are Grieving *132*
When Someone is Dying 134
   To the Person Who is Dying *134*
   To Someone Whose Loved One is Dying *137*
Suicide...138
   If Someone Threatens Suicide *138*
   When Someone Dies by Suicide *142*
Miscarriage 144
Death of a Full-Term Baby, or Child 147
Anniversaries, Holidays, Birthdays, and Special Occasions
   after the Death of a Loved One...148
   When Someone is Facing a Significant Date after the Death
     of a Loved One *149*
   When You are Facing a Significant Date Without a
     Loved One *151*
Death of a Pet..152

Chapter Six: Illness, Injury, and Disability 155
   Acute (Short) Illness or Injury 155
     To the Ill or Injured Person...*155*
     To the Spouse/Close Relatives..*157*
   During a Lengthy Recovery, at Home or in the Hospital 161
     To the Person Who is Ill or Injured....................................*163*
   Chronic (Long-Term) Illness 164
     When Someone is Diagnosed with a Chronic Illness........*164*
     Ongoing—Weeks and Months after the Diagnosis *166*
     When a Child has a Chronic Illness..................................*167*
   When Someone Has a Severe/Terminal Illness 169
   Babies and Children With Special Needs or a Disability 171
     When a Baby is Born with Special Needs or
       a Disability..*171*

    If Your Baby has Special Needs *173*
    An Older Child with a Disability *174*

Chapter Seven: Various Sticky, Tricky, Uncomfortable Situations **177**
    General Guidelines for Telling Someone Something They Don't Want to Hear 178
    Two Friends Have a Falling Out 179
    If Someone Asks You for a Job Reference 180
    If a Friend is in an Abusive Relationship 181
    If a Friend has been Sexually Assaulted 183
    When a Friend is Depressed 184
    If You Suspect a Friend is Addicted 186
    After a Friend or Acquaintance has Attempted Suicide 187
    Unexpected Pregnancy 188
        When a Friend's Unmarried Child is Pregnant *188*
        If a Friend is Unexpectedly Pregnant *190*
    Secrets 191
        Revealing a Secret from Your Past *191*
        When a Friend Shares a Secret *193*
    Invitations and Get-togethers 195
        When Someone Asks for an Invitation *195*
        If Someone Wants to Invite Another Guest to Attend with Him *196*
    Asking Awkward Questions 197
    Foot-in-Mouth Disease—When You Accidentally put Your Foot in Your Mouth 199
    Is it Good or Bad News? 201
        When You Don't Know if Someone's News is Good or Bad *201*
        If Someone Misinterprets Your News *202*
    Problems with Neighbors 203

Chapter Seven: Encouraging Words **205**
    When a Friend is Making a Big Decision 205
    If a Family Member is Being Deployed 206
    Disappointment After Working Hard for Something 208

Compliments 209
   Giving Compliments..*209*
   Accepting a Compliment *212*
Acknowledging a Difficult Decision 213

Acknowledgements 215

Appendix...217
   Asking the Holy Spirit to Guide Your Words 217
   Tone of Voice (Using Tone of Voice to Your Advantage)......218
   10 Worst Things to Say in Any Situation..............................219
   10 Best Things to Say When You Don't Know What
      to Say 220

Index...221

Chapter One

Everyday Situations

This chapter covers quandaries you'll face in everyday life whether at work, school, home, church, with friends, or a large get-together. When you are prepared for these situations, you'll be better able to respond appropriately.

Advice

When Someone Asks for Your Advice
When you are asked for advice, be honest with the person who asked for it. Be prepared to explain your advice, especially if it's not the advice your friend wanted to hear. Here are some ways to reply.

What to Say
- *"I've been thinking about your situation, and since you asked for advice, here's what I think and why."*
- *"Here's my advice—I'm not sure if it's what you expect, but it's the best advice I have."*
- *"I'm not sure how to respond to that. I'll think about it and get back to you."*

If the person asks for advice about a minor matter, or you don't want to share your opinion, say something like:
- *"That is something I know you will come to the right decision about."*

- *"I'll listen to you talk through your problem, but this is something you need to decide. I will support your decision."*
- *"I don't like to give advice, but I'll listen. Sometimes just talking about it helps clarify your options."*

If an issue is complicated or you don't feel qualified to give advice, say:
- *"A counselor could give you much better advice than I could on that issue!"*
- *"Have you thought about talking with your priest or a counselor about that? I think he would be better able to help you come to the right decision."*
- *"That's a really tough situation and I just don't know what to suggest. A professional could give you better advice than I could."*
- A few days or weeks later, you might want to ask, *"Since we talked, how are things going?"*

What Not to Say
- *"Here's what you need to do . . . "*
- *"There's only one answer, and I have it!"*

What to Do
- Pray for guidance about what advice to give, and for your friend to make a wise decision.
- Listen to your friend; sometimes just talking through a dilemma will make her options clear to her.

Don't . . .
- . . . ask the person if she took your advice.
- . . . become upset if she does not take your advice.

Giving Unasked for Advice

You might feel obligated to give advice (even if you're not asked for it) if you feel someone close to you is making a life-changing mistake or is in danger.

Before you give unsolicited advice, consider your motives. Do you want to give advice just so your friend will give you all the details of her dilemma? Do you feel superior because you have faced and 'solved' the problem she's facing? Keep your advice to yourself unless you truly have your friend's best interests in mind. Be aware that giving unasked-for advice might cause tension between the two of you. If you decide to share your opinions, here are some ways to approach the subject.

What to Say
- *"I'm worried about you, and as a friend I feel like I have to tell you . . ."*
- *"I know you didn't ask me, but I was in a similar situation, and here's what I did and why."*
- *"I feel very strongly about what is going on in your life, and I'd like to offer you this advice."*
- *"You are a wonderful friend, and I want to say this because I care so much about you . . ."*
- If your friend gets angry, say, *"I'm sorry I interfered. I meant to help, not make it worse. I've told you what I think, and I won't say any more about it."* (You do not have to apologize for what you said.)

What Not to Say
- *"You're making a huge mistake—here's what you need to do!"*
- *"You'd be really dumb not to take my advice."*
- *"I don't know how you managed to get yourself into this mess, but I do know what you need to do to get out of it."*

What to Do
- Pray before you give unsolicited advice, and if you decide that doing so is God's will, pray for the right words.
- Make sure you have all the facts before you make a judgment about what you think the person should do.
- Give any advice with the realization that the person you're giving it to might become angry or upset with you for doing so.

Don't . . .
- . . . apologize for your point of view.
- . . . project an attitude of being superior to the person you're giving the advice to.
- . . . get upset if the person doesn't take your advice.

Asking for Advice

Before you ask for advice, consider your motives. If you're looking for a certain answer, perhaps you've already made up your mind and don't really need anyone's advice. Remember that the person you ask might expect you to follow his advice and be hurt or angry if you don't. Here are a few ways to approach the subject.

What to Say
- *"I'm in a difficult position, and I want to ask for your advice."*
- *"I know you've been in this situation before . . . what did you do when . . . "*
- *"I'd like you to tell me what you think about something that's going on in my life. Here's my dilemma . . . "*
- *"I'm not sure what I'm going to do, or if I'll take your advice, but I'd like to know what you'd do in my situation."*

What Not to Say
- *"You've just got to help me solve this problem!"*
- In reply to a suggestion, *"That would be a dumb thing to do!"*

What to Do
- Ask for advice from people who share your values.
- Include all the details of the situation when asking someone for advice (even if the details show you've made bad decisions).
- Carefully think through (and pray about) any advice before you act on it.
- Thank the person for his advice.

Don't . . .
- . . . say you'll take the advice if you have no intention of doing so.

- ... take advice that's not right for you, no matter who gives it to you.

If You Receive Unasked for Advice

What to Say
- *"Thanks for your thoughts."*
- *"Well, that is one solution . . . "*
- *"I'm not sure if that's the right solution for me, but thank you for thinking of me."*
- *"I'm glad that worked for you, but I don't think it's right for me."*

If you're asked if you took the advice, be truthful:
- *"I'm still thinking about how to handle it."*
- *"I've come up with something that I think will work better for me."*
- *"That's great advice! I'll try it."*
- *"The problem is resolved; thanks for your thoughts."*
- *"Thanks so much for your advice—it worked!"*

What Not to Say
- *"I'll do that!"* (if you have no intention of doing so).

What to Do
- Pray for the wisdom to do what's right in your situation.
- Reply kindly yet firmly to the person giving the advice.

Don't . . .
- . . . take advice that's not right for you, no matter who gives it to you.
- . . . promise to take the advice if you don't plan to do so.
- . . . lie about having taken the advice if you did not.

Favors

Offering a Favor

Remember that the people who need a favor the most are often reluctant, embarrassed, or ashamed to have to ask. In times of crisis, people might not even think to ask for help. Be alert to situations where your offer of a favor could bless someone.

What to Say
- "I would like to do _____ for you."
- "What can I do that would help you the most?"
- "I will come over tomorrow and help you clean your house."
- "I can pick up the kids and watch them tomorrow; when I bring them back I'll bring supper, if that's OK with you."

Offer to do specific tasks, especially if the person is in the midst of a crisis;
- "Do you have someone to stay with the baby during the funeral? I will be available."
- "Can I pick up some groceries for you? What do you need most?"
- "Are there any phone calls I can make?"

What Not to Say
- "What can I do for you?" (Offering to do something specific is better.)
- "Let me know if you need anything." (The person might not feel comfortable asking you for something, or might not even know what to ask for.)

What to Do
- Offer to do specific tasks that the person might be too overwhelmed to do, or even think of asking you to do.
- If you know the person well enough to know that it won't upset or offend her, just do what needs to be done, like laundry, cooking, or cleaning.

Don't . . .
- . . . do so much that the person feels uncomfortable with all that you are doing for her or becomes dependent on your constant help.
- . . . insist on doing a favor if the person strenuously objects or repeatedly tells you not to.

How to Say "No;" Turning Down a Request for a Favor

There are many reasons to say *"yes"* when asked for a favor. In many cases, it is the 'right'—the Christian—thing to do. Doing a favor is a chance to use your skills and strengths to help someone, and may be an opportunity for you to learn something new or even make a new friend.

However, if doing a favor for someone would cause excessive stress or inconvenience for you or your family, it's OK to say *"no"*. It's also OK to refuse for moral reasons, if you feel the person is taking advantage of you, or 'just because'. You are not obligated to give a reason, but depending on your relationship with the person requesting the favor, you might want to (if the person is a casual acquaintance, you don't have to share details; if you're turning down a close friend or family member, you might want to give more of an explanation).

Here is a selection of answers that should encompass most of your reasons for saying *"no"*. Pick the one that works for you!

What to Say
- *"I'm sorry, it just won't work for me."* (You don't have to go into the reasons why it won't work for you.)
- *"I can't be the chairman this year, but ask me again next year."* (Only say this if you mean it, because the person *will* ask you next year!)
- *"We already have plans for that day. Perhaps I can help you another time."* (You are not obligated to tell the person what your plans are.)
- *"Thank you for asking me, but teaching is just not one of my gifts and I don't feel comfortable doing it."*

- *"I just can't commit to anything else right now. I don't want to be able to say I'd do it and then have to back out, so I have to say 'no' this time."*
- If you are not interested in ever joining a certain organization or helping with a particular charity or project, make it clear in a kind way; *"I'm just not interested, but thank you for thinking of me."*
- *"I don't have the time to do a good job on that now, and you deserve to have it done by someone who has the time to devote to it. I have to say "no" this time."*

If you need some time to consider the request, say;
- *"What are the dates? I need to check with my husband to see if we have plans."*
- *"I need to think about that; when do you need to know?"*

Sometimes you can find a compromise;
- *"I can watch your children until noon, but not all day."*
- *"I can help on Monday, but that's the only day I'm free next week."*
- *"I don't want to be in charge of Vacation Bible School, but I can make phone calls and help on sign-up day."*

Don't compromise your values and do a favor if someone asks you to do something unethical such as lie or steal. If you choose to point out that what she is asking you to do is immoral or illegal, be prepared for a defensive reaction.
Here are some suggestions.
- *"I'm not comfortable lying about where you are or who you're with, so I can't cover for you."*
- *"My conscience would bother me if I signed a sheet for expenses you didn't really have, even if the boss never finds out."*
- *"I don't agree with what you are doing. I will not be a part of it, so can't do what you are asking."*

What Not to Say
- *"Um, er, well ... maybe ... let me think about it."* (If your answer is *"no,"* tell the person right away.)
- *"I can't believe you'd ask me to do something so stupid!"* (Respond with kindness.)
- *"I think that's the day I have to brush and floss my cat's teeth."* (Instead of a silly excuse that your acquaintance will easily see through, tell the truth about why you are turning down her request.)

What to Do
- Pray for guidance if your answer to the request is not obvious or clear.
- Allow a silence after you've given your answer; the other person may hope you'll be eager to break the silence by giving more details, and then agree to do it 'after all'.
- Realize that you are not obligated to share the details behind a *"no"* answer. If the person making the request asks for more details about your plans, just repeat your original answer, several times if necessary!

Don't ...
- ... automatically say *"no"* to something new, or something you've said *"no"* to in the past. God might be leading you in a new direction; follow His guidance.
- ... say *"yes"* to something if you feel led to say *"no."* You will resent agreeing to something that's not right for you.
- ... allow anyone to change your mind after a *"no"* answer.
- ... be afraid to change your answer to *"yes"* if you gave your *"no"* answer too fast, and feel led to later agree to the request.

Asking for a Favor
Sometimes it's hard to ask for a favor, but when you truly need one, friends will probably be more than happy to help you out if they can. Remember that it is a blessing to be able to help someone; when you ask for help, you are giving that person the opportunity to bless you, which in turn is a blessing to her.

What to Say
- *"I have a favor to ask you, but I understand if you can't help me."*
- *"It's difficult for me to ask for this, but it's really important. Please be honest if it's not something you want to do."*
- *"Could you help me out? I was wondering if you would . . . "*
- *"Would you have the time to look over my resume' and give me any suggestions as to how to put it together?"*
- If you feel it's appropriate, provide details; *"My husband and I are going through a tough time. We're seeing a counselor tomorrow afternoon; could you watch the kids for a few hours?"*

Consider a trade-off:
- *"As a favor, could you watch my kids Saturday morning? In turn, I'll watch your kids any morning next week."*

What Not to Say
- *"What are you doing next weekend?"* (Don't put the person on the spot about their plans before asking for your favor.)
- *"Since I helped you with that favor last year, now it's your turn. I need you to . . . "*

What to Do
- Pray about who to ask to do the favor for you.
- Explain what the favor is, when you need it by, and other details, when you ask for the favor.
- Be clear about when you'd like an answer so you can make other arrangements if necessary.

Don't . . .
- . . . imply that the person "owes" you, even if you have done many favors for him.
- . . . press for an immediate answer unless you really need the answer right away, and if so, apologize for the short notice.
- . . . be vague about what the favor is.

Accepting a Favor

When someone offers a favor, remember that it is a blessing to be able to help someone. Allow someone to bless you, and be blessed in return, by accepting the favor he or she is offering.

What to Say
- "Thank you so much for offering—perfect timing!"
- "Thank you so much!"
- "It is just what we needed—thank you."
- "You are such a blessing to me. Thank you."

What Not to Say
- "I just can't stand to be obligated to someone."

What to Do
- Thank God that the person came into your life when you needed him.
- Send a thank-you note or take the person a small token of your appreciation—homemade cookies or flowers from your garden, for example.

Don't . . .
- . . . automatically turn down a favor; accept it if you need it!

Turning Down a Favor You're Offered

Sometimes there are good reasons to turn down the offer of a favor. If you know from experience that the person offering the favor has ulterior motives, will demand payback (on his or her terms), or places conditions on his or her favors, it's best not to accept the favor.

What to Say
- "Thanks for offering, but I have something else in mind."
- "I'm not comfortable borrowing money from you or receiving it as a gift, but thanks for the offer."
- "When I accept a favor from you, you expect payback on your terms and I am uncomfortable with that. Thanks anyway."

- *"I know from experience that your favors have strings attached and I do not want to be in that position. No thanks."*

What Not to Say
- *"You're such a manipulator. You never do anything without strings attached, so don't even offer."* (Using words like this could escalate the situation. Say this in a kinder way.)

What to Do
- Be kind, yet firm, in turning down the offer.

Don't . . .
- . . . be rude or mean when turning down the offer.
- . . . let yourself be bullied into accepting a favor you don't want.

Perhaps the person offering the favor is not the right one to help you; you don't want someone who can't even balance her checkbook to help you with your taxes for example, or someone who has not finished a household project in five years to lay your kitchen tile. Perhaps the timing is wrong, or for another reason you're just not comfortable with your friend's offer. Here are some kind replies to the offer of a favor you don't want.

What to Say
- *"Can I take a rain check on that?"* (Say this only if you truly want the favor, just at a later time.)
- *"Oh, I just couldn't ask that of a friend!"*
- *"That is too much of an imposition for you."*
- *"What would help me even more is . . . "* (Ask for something your friend is qualified to give or do, or something that would truly help.)
- *"It means so much to me that you would even offer, but we've already hired a professional to do the work."*

What Not to Say
- *"Well . . . er . . . um . . . "* (When you know your answer will be *"no,"* tell the person immediately.)

What to Do
- Be kind, yet firm, in your refusal.

Don't . . .
- . . . allow the person to do the favor if you truly do not want him to.

Personal Beliefs and Lifestyle Choices

Expressing Yours

Every person and family is unique in regards to its beliefs and practices of day-to-day life. What people eat, wear, do in their free time, how late the kids stay up, if they recycle, how much TV they watch, whether they send their kids to public, private, parochial school or home school, if they do or don't drink alcohol or smoke, and countless other details, make every family distinctive.

For the most part, these personal quirks and details of family life are unnoticed by others, or are accepted as just part of that family's lifestyle. Occasionally you might be asked about, or even challenged on, details of your lifestyle. Here are a few non-confrontational replies.

What to Say
- *"I don't eat sugary snacks. I don't feel good after eating them, so I avoid them."*
- *"We don't like to expose our kids to violence or sexually explicit movies, so we don't watch them."*
- *"We've decided that our kids won't watch TV during the day."*
- *"I just don't eat eggs."*
- *"I've studied different diets, and decided vegetarianism is right for me and my family."*

- *"I recycle whenever I can." "I don't recycle because there are no collection centers near here."*
- *"For our kids, private/parochial/public/home school is the best option for their education."*
- *"That's just one of my quirks."*
- *"It's part of my lifestyle to do it that way."*

What Not to Say:
- *"If you were responsible, you'd do what I do."* (Being judgmental or harsh won't encourage anyone to follow your lifestyle.)
- *"You really should be responsible and . . ."*
- *"You should never/always. . ."*

What to Do
- Be matter-of-fact about your beliefs and practices.
- Say these things in a matter-of-fact, non-judgmental manner. You don't have to give detailed reasons for your beliefs (you don't have to give any reasons at all!).
- If you want to educate others on aspects of your lifestyle, use solid information, not scare tactics.

Don't . . .
- . . . be in-your-face or pushy about your beliefs and practices.
- . . . be judgmental about others' practices or habits.

Others' Lifestyles

Respect others' lifestyle choices, even if you don't choose to live that way. It's OK to ask about a specific aspect of their lifestyle, if you are truly interested and don't just want to try to convince them that your way is 'better'. Here are several ways to reply if someone tries to persuade you to adapt their lifestyle.

What to Say
- *"I'm glad that works so well for you, but it's just not for us."*
- *"I respect your beliefs, but do not agree. Here's why . . ."*
- *"That's a pretty intense topic for here and now—let's talk about something else."*

- *"Thanks for telling me how you came to believe what you do."*
- *"I guess we'll just have to agree to disagree on this issue."*

If you believe that what someone is doing is potentially harmful, you can say,
- *"Have you talked with your doctor about going on that diet?"*
- *"I've read recently that some of those supplements contain dangerous amounts of the minerals and lead and can be dangerous. Have you heard that?"*
- *"Are you worried about the recent research that has shown that to be potentially harmful?"*

If your friend is doing something that is against your religious beliefs, say,
- *"That goes against what the Bible says. Can I talk with you about why I do not agree with what you are doing?"*

What Not to Say
- *"You must be crazy to believe/eat/think that!"*
- *"I can't believe you've been taken in by that nonsense."*
- *"God won't love you anymore if you don't stop."*

What to Do
- Remember that God accepts our differences, unless they go against His word. Show the same accommodation for your friends, family, co-workers, and acquaintances.
- Acknowledge others' beliefs and respect them, and try to accommodate them if it is not extremely inconvenient or contrary to your beliefs. If a vegetarian friend is coming for supper, make sure there are one or more dishes she can eat. Make sure non-alcoholic beverages are available for those who do not care to drink alcohol. If someone recycles, put trash in appropriate receptacles at her home.

Don't . . .
- . . . point out someone's beliefs or practices publicly. For example, if someone who doesn't drink alcohol is at a party, don't announce it to a group of people.
- . . . try to trick someone into eating, drinking, or doing something that they usually do not do. It is disrespectful, and can be dangerous if the person is not eating or drinking or doing something due to health reasons.
- . . . mock someone's beliefs or practices.

Religion and Politics

People's core values and morals are usually based at least partly on religious and/or political beliefs. Almost everyone has passionate feelings about some aspects of religion and/or politics, and since there are (at least) two sides to every issue, there are also many heated discussions about these issues.

Here are several situations in which you might be, and possible replies:

What to Say

To start a discussion:
- *"What did you think of the election?"*
- *"What are your thoughts on _____?"*
- *"I'd like to hear your point of view; will you hear my thoughts too?"*

You can disagree with actions of a person or group by saying,
- *"I do not agree with the decision to . . ."*
- *"I think they should have handled it differently . . ."*

At an occasion or in a setting where a serious discussion is inappropriate—a funeral, for example—or when you can tell that continuing the conversation will lead to an argument, you might say:

- *"I think we're on the opposite side of that issue and this isn't really an appropriate place to discuss it, so let's talk about something else."*
- With a smile, say, *"You're sitting at the table with three people who happen to take the opposite point of view! Let's talk about something else."*

If the situation is escalating, diffuse it;
- *"I can see that we have very different thoughts about that, and that's what's great about America—we can all have our own point of view. How about this nice weather we're having?"*
- *"I don't think any of us know all the details about that issue . . . let's just talk about something else. What did you think about the championship game last week?"*

At some time, you will probably be in a situation where you want to talk about your religious beliefs or political views. Remember that the way you present your beliefs will influence how the other person receives them—if you are pushy, strident, critical of his or her beliefs, or confrontational in expressing your own beliefs, the person you are trying to convince might not even hear your message, let alone consider your point of view. Keep your voice calm and expression friendly. You might say;
- *"In our church, we believe _____; in contrast, your church believes _____."*
- *"Our religion teaches _____; how does that compare to what your religion teaches?"*
- *"I think the neatest part about what I believe is . . ."*
- *"Here's why I've taken my view of this issue . . ."*
- *"My political party is in favor of _____, while yours is against it."*

What Not to Say
- *"I'm right; you're wrong."*
- *"Your religion is really weird."*
- *"Your political party is always for the wrong thing."*
- *"If you believe what you do, you're stupid."*

What to Do
- If you do decide to get into a conversation about religion or politics, make sure you truly want to talk about the issue, not just argue about it, and are able to clearly state and explain your position, as well as calmly listen to another point of view.
- Always remain calm when presenting your beliefs. If a particular issue comes up frequently, consider writing out and practicing the important points so you can present them clearly and calmly.
- Calmly listen to the other person's point of view, without interrupting.
- If the situation is escalating, diffuse it by making one of the comments listed previously, or walking away. If you become angry, you will not convince anyone of your point of view, and might give the person a bad impression of the beliefs that are most important to you.
- Many people know very little about politics or particular religious beliefs or practices. If you are well-informed and able to express your views calmly and clearly, consider yourself an educator and use your knowledge to share your beliefs and clear up common misconceptions.

Don't . . .
- . . . use inflammatory words like 'stupid', 'idiotic', or anything demeaning.
- . . . discuss a controversial topic if the other person is very argumentative or inebriated.
- . . . use absolutes (always, never) when describing your own, or the opposing, point of view. There are almost always exceptions.
- . . . have religious or political debates in an inappropriate setting, like at a funeral.

If Someone Insults Something Important to You

Whether it's a group or organization you belong to, a hobby you enjoy, or something you believe in, it is hurtful (and annoying!) when someone criticizes, laughs at, or insults something important to you. Use these responses to express your feelings.

What to Say
- *"That might be the case in another group, but it is not true of our group!"*
- *"Why do you feel that way about my hobby?"*
- *"What makes you say that?"* (perhaps you can correct the person's misperceptions).
- *"That's a very hurtful thing to say about something that is so important to me."*

What Not to Say
- *"You don't know what you're talking about."*
- *"You're pretty dumb if you don't want to be part of my group."*

What to Do
- Ask the person why she said what she did; maybe she heard false information, or if she's criticizing a group, perhaps she had a bad experience with the group. If this is the case, politely correct the misconceptions.
- Invite the person to a meeting of your group.
- Educate the person about your hobby.
- Be a positive example of your group.
- Give a personal account of your own experience to show why it is important/significant to you.

Don't . . .
- . . . try to convince someone you are correct by over-reacting.

Gossip

Gossip seems harmless, but if you've ever been the victim of gossip, you know how hurtful words can be. God considers it a serious enough topic that there are many Bible verses warning against it (among them Lev. 19:16, Pro. 26:20, 22, and Eph. 4:29). Despite His warnings, it's easy to get caught up in gossip almost without realizing it. If you are with someone, or a group of some-ones, and gossip begins, here are a few ways to stop it.

What to Say
- *"I would not want people talking about the private details of my life, especially if there's no way they could know what's really going on. Let's give him the benefit of the doubt and not speculate."*
- Try humor; *"Gosh, I'd hate to hear what you say about me when I'm not here! Let's change the subject—how do you like the weather?"*
- *"My New Year's resolution is to only say good things about other people. Do you want to join me in that resolution?"*
- *"I don't think it's fair to talk about her when she's not here to give her side of what happened."* Then change the subject; *"So, how was your weekend?"*
- *"Oh, my, look at the time! I've got to get back to work on that project."*
- If someone tries to tantalize you by hinting that she knows the details of the latest scandal, reply, *"Well, I guess we'll all know soon enough, won't we?"* and change the subject.

Have you ever caught yourself in the center of a group of people who are waiting to hear the juicy gossip that's about to come out of your mouth? Here's how to rescue yourself from that situation.
- *"Wait a minute—I know better than to spread gossip. Let's change the subject—what are you doing this weekend?"*
- *"Oh, no, I just heard my mom's voice saying, "If you can't say something nice, don't say anything at all," I better listen to her!"*

- Dramatically clap your hand over your mouth and say, *"A very non-Christian thing almost came out of my mouth—good thing my conscience is attached to my hand!"*

What Not to Say
- *"Oh, please, tell me all the juicy details!"*
- *"Let me tell you everything I know!"*

What to Do
- Talk in a serious tone of voice, with a solemn look on your face, when you try to stop gossip.
- Walk away if gossip starts, or continues after you've tried to change the subject.

Don't . . .
- . . . even listen to gossip; by doing so you are saying with your actions that it's OK to gossip.
- . . . be embarrassed about not fulfilling your promise of juicy gossip.
- . . . ignore gossip if it is about a friend (see next section).

Should You Tell Someone She's Being Gossiped About?
Immediately refute any gossip about someone else, that you know to be false. Here are a few ways to do so.

What to Say
- *"I am her friend and I know that is absolutely untrue."*
- *"I would not want people talking about the private details of my life, especially if there's no way they could know what's really going on. Let's give him the benefit of the doubt and not speculate."*

What Not to Say
- *"Oh, what else did you hear? Tell me all the details!"*

What to Do
- Walk away if the gossip continues.

Don't . . .
- . . . repeat the gossip.

Before you tell someone they are the subject of gossip, ask yourself if doing so will help that person. If what is being said is harmless—*"What a haircut!"* or, *"I wouldn't carry around a purse like that!"*—there is no reason to repeat it to her; it would just be hurtful and there's nothing she did to cause the gossip or can do to prevent it.

However, if your friend's actions are fueling gossip, you might want to draw her attention to her actions and the impression they are giving. In this case, not telling her could cause harm by hurting her reputation or family or even jeopardizing her job. Tell her gently, in private, how her actions appear. Be prepared for her to be upset, but reassure her you are telling her because of your concern for her well-being.

What to Say
- *"I know you're friends with the boss; in the cafeteria yesterday several people were speculating that you're having an affair with him. Of course I assured them that you are not, but I wanted you to know how your actions around him look to some people."*
- *"I don't know why your friendship with Chris ended, but she is saying that you borrowed money and did not pay it back. That does not sound like something you would do! Do you mind telling me what really happened so I can set people straight?"*

What Not to Say
- *"Tell me all the details of what happened with you and the boss, so I can pass them on."*

What to Do
- Pray that your friend would realize how her actions appear.
- Reassure your friend of your support and friendship.

Don't . . .
- . . . share the names of the people doing the gossiping.
- . . . repeat the gossip to anyone else!

Losing a Job

When Someone Loses His Job

A person's job is a part of his or her identity, so losing a job is difficult for emotional reasons, not just financial ones. Here are some suggestions for helping a friend through this experience.

What to Say
- *"I'm so sorry!"*
- *"How are you doing?"*
- *"Did you know it was coming?"*
- *"What's next?"* (The person might be planning to go back to school, look for a job in a completely different area, or open his own business rather than looking for another job right away. Ask, so you can offer your help and support as you're able to.)
- *"What can I do to help?"*
- *"How is the job search going?"* (if the person is searching for another job).

What Not to Say
- *"What kind of severance pay did you get?"*
- *"I knew that was a bad job for you."*
- *"How will you pay for rent and groceries, now that you don't have an income?"*

What to Do
- Pass on job information, as appropriate. For example, tell your friend if a suitable position is available in your company, or if you see a promising job advertised in the want-ads.
- Be sensitive about asking questions like, *"Did you send in that resume'?" "What are you doing today?"* The person might

appreciate your friendly concern, but could see your questions as implying that he is not doing enough.
- Offer your help in any area of expertise; writing or reviewing a resume', coaching the person on interview techniques, and so on. If you expect to be paid for typing a resume', make that clear before you do it. For example, mention, *"I wish I could do this for you for free, but I have bills! I will do it for half price, which is . . . "* If you are doing it as a gift, make that clear, also. *"If you'd like, I'll be happy to type up your resume' for you, no charge. Just spread the word if you're happy with my work!"*
- Let the person know with your words and actions that he is still your friend and your friendship isn't based on him having a job.
- Be encouraging, but realistic, as your friend searches for a job or a new direction. If he wants to apply for a job you feel is totally inappropriate, ask questions which will lead him to think about why the job might not be appropriate for him.

Don't . . .
- . . . make any discouraging comments about the job market, insurance, his bills, and so on. You can be sure these issues are already a worry to your jobless friend!
- . . . project your expectations on the person who has lost his or her job. He might not go about a job hunt as you would, or might choose to take a completely different path than you deem a good choice. Your job is to be supportive. If you feel he is making a mistake, ask questions about what you're worried about and gently voice your concerns.

If You've Lost Your Job

What to Say
- *"Would you please pray for . . . "*
- *"It was quite a shock to learn that I didn't have a job after next week!"*
- *"I knew changes were coming, so it wasn't a complete surprise."*

When people ask what they can do to help, tell them!
- *"May I use your name as a reference when I fill out job applications?"*
- *"I would like to get my resume' to the right person in your office. To whom should I send it?"*
- *"Would you have time to take a look at my resume' and give me suggestions to improve it?"*
- *"I'm thinking of opening my own home business. You've been running your home business for several years; could we get together to talk about what it takes?"*

What Not to Say
- *"I know you can get me a job at your company if you really want to."*

What to Do
- Remember to thank anyone who helps you, preferably in writing. If what they've done to help (like type your resume') is part of their business, be sure to pass the information on to anyone you meet that could use the service.
- Only tell people what you want to about losing a job; it's not necessary to divulge details if you don't want to.

Don't . . .
- . . . say anything negative about your old job or boss, or the people you worked with. You might be complaining to a potential employer!
- . . . talk negatively about your job search—that negativity will affect your attitude.

Money Problems

Offering Help to Someone Who is Having Money Problems
Money problems are common; we all have them at some point in our lives. If a friend or acquaintance is having money problems, here are some ways to offer your support without causing embar-

rassment. (If your friend has frequent money problems, of her own making, see "When Someone Won't Take Responsibility for His or Her Problems," in Chapter 3.)

What to Say
- *"Everyone has money problems at some point; we had a tough time a few years ago, so I understand."*
- If you'd like to go somewhere with a friend, but know her finances are tight, say, *"Let's go to the craft fair this weekend—my treat!"* or, *"Let's go out for lunch next week—on me!"*
- To offer help without embarrassing the recipient, say, *"I went on a baking kick and made four casseroles today; here's one of them. I thought you might enjoy a day of not having to plan and cook supper." "I was cleaning out my freezer and found some extra hamburger. We'll never eat it all, so here is some for you." "Here are some of my kids' outgrown clothes; I think some of them will fit your kids."*
- If the person seems embarrassed by your offer, say something like, *"When I was having money troubles, someone helped me out and I promised to pass on the favor when I could. Now I am so glad I can help you! And when you are able to, I hope you'll help someone who needs it, too."*

What Not to Say
- *"What did you do to get yourself into this mess?"*
- *"Here's what you need to do to fix it . . . "*
- *"You shouldn't have bought so many clothes/such a big house/a fancy car!"*

What to Do
- Pray for the wisdom to know what you can do to best help your friend.
- Offer to help the person find a financial counselor.
- If you know of a money-making opportunity (a new job, temporary work, a part-time job), mention it, but without the expectation that the person "should" take the job.

- Suggest possible ways for the person to bring in extra money; garage sales, selling things on E-bay, and so on. Offer to help if you're able and qualified.
- Pass on information about low-cost housing, low-cost insurance, special dental and medical programs for people with a low income, etc. as appropriate for the situation. Be tactful and matter-of-fact about it; *"I heard about this great program for insurance for kids of parents who are having financial problems. Here's the phone number." "I read that the dental college is offering free check-ups for kids next week. Here is the phone number."*
- Give a gift card to a grocery store or shoe store; consider sending it anonymously if you think the person will be hesitant to accept your help.
- Realize that ongoing money problems usually involve other personal issues, and just giving the person money won't solve the problem.
- If your friend asks for a loan, think carefully about the implications of that loan.

Don't . . .
- . . . encourage someone to spend money she does not have, by saying, *"Oh, come on and treat yourself, you deserve it!"* or, *"Blowing your paycheck won't make a difference in the long run; just do it!"*
- . . . offer food, clothing, money (as a loan or gift), or anything else, unless you are able to do so freely, without judging how the person uses what you give him.
- . . . offer to loan or give money to someone without prayer and careful consideration.
- . . . get involved in helping a friend with her money problems to the extent of shortchanging your own family.
- . . . insist that a friend take your financial advice, or use your financial solutions.
- . . . question or judge purchases your friend makes; perhaps they were made with a gift card or in exchange for something she returned. What she buys is none of your business.

- ... cosign a loan without knowing exactly what your obligations are in doing so. If you cosign a loan and the person who took out the loan doesn't pay, you are legally obligated to make the payments. Make sure you know what you're getting into!

If You are Having Money Problems

What to Say
- *"We're a little short financially this month; instead of 'girls' night out' with a movie and dinner, how about coming to my house to make ice cream sundaes?"*
- If you're shopping with friends, and they urge you to buy something; *"I'm just window shopping today,"* or, *"I'm really picky today—I'm not going to buy anything unless it's absolutely perfect!"* or, *"Any extra money I have goes to pay bills and pay off our credit cards."*
- If you are given financial advice, leads on a job opening, or other information that helps your situation, reply with, *"Thanks for the information!"*

What Not to Say
- *"Gee, must be nice to have enough money to buy anything you want when you're shopping."*
- *"You would never understand not spending; you've never had to worry!"* (Avoid lashing out at people who at the time don't appear to be having money problems.)
- When you're given advice or information, *"That would never work; what a dumb idea!"*

What to Do
- Be matter-of-fact about your money problems.
- If a friend knows of your tight finances and offers to treat you to a movie, accept her generous gesture with the intent of reciprocating when you can, or passing on the help to someone else when you are able to. Just say, *"Thanks, I really appreciate it."* (Remember that it is a blessing and a joy for your friend to be able to give to you!)

- Graciously accept offers of food or other items you need.

Don't . . .
- . . . complain about your lack of funds, dwell on, place blame for, or give endless details of your money problems.
- . . . spend money you don't have, even if you're pressured to.

Spouse Bashing

When you're with friends or a group of people, the conversation often turns to spouses and their shortcomings, and then further deteriorates into a session of spouse bashing. While you may enjoy having the momentary attention of having the 'worst spouse,' criticizing your spouse can erode your relationship with him or her.

Here are some responses that will turn the conversation in a more positive direction.

What to Say
- *"I hate to criticize; after all, I'm certainly not perfect either!"*
- *"I am so blessed; my husband took the kids to the park so I could have a nap yesterday."*
- *"On our last anniversary, my husband and I promised to never criticize or complain about each other to anyone else, but instead to talk with each other if there are problems."*
- *"My wife made me a wonderful supper last night, and afterwards, rubbed my back! I love her so much."*
- *"I made a resolution to not talk to anyone but my spouse about any complaints about him; do you want to join me on that resolution?"*

What Not to Say
- *"Wow, your husband sounds like a real loser!"*
- *"Let me tell you how much worse my wife is!"*
- *"I wouldn't put up with that behavior—tell her to shape up or ship out."*

What to Do
- Talk over problems with your spouse, not someone outside of your marriage.
- If you need to talk with someone about small irritations or problems, do so to a close friend who shares your beliefs and will encourage you to improve your marriage, not add to the spouse bashing.
- After you've talked with your friend, make an effort to talk about the positive attributes of your spouse.
- When you are in a group and spouse-bashing begins, pray for the right words to say, or the strength to walk away from the conversation.
- Consider making a commitment with your spouse to only say flattering and positive things about each other in public.
- Pray for your spouse; pray to see his or her strong points, not weaknesses.
- Walk away if the spouse-bashing continues.

Don't . . .
- . . . join in by criticizing your spouse, or someone else's, no matter how tempting it is to do so.

Sexist/Racist/Bigoted Remarks or Jokes

Stereotypical, racist, bigoted, or sexist comments about any group of people are never OK, but unfortunately are a common occurrence. Some people are offended by jokes about blonds or people of a certain age or ethnic or religious group, and some are not. Before you tell a joke targeting a racial, ethnic, social, or religious group of people, ask yourself if you would think it was funny if you belonged to that group. If you would be offended, or if you sense someone in the group would be offended, don't tell the joke.

Use the following remarks if unacceptable comments are made.

What to Say
- *"That is a very sexist comment!"*

- *"Remarks like that are not appropriate."*
- *"That generalization is untrue for most of the group of people you are talking about."*
- After a stereotypical comment; *"Do you have facts to back that up?"* or, *"Actually statistics show that . . . "*
- *"I really don't like jokes like that. Can we please talk about something else?"*

What Not to Say
- *" . . . um, er, you know, that's not the nicest thing to say and maybe we shouldn't talk about people that way, I think . . . "*

What to Do
- Say a quick prayer asking God to give you the right words to diffuse the situation.
- Say your comments in a calm, firm voice, with a serious expression on your face, and then change the subject to something neutral, like the weather or another generic topic.

Don't . . .
- . . . apologize for your beliefs about not making disparaging remarks.

Uncomfortable Situations or When You are Shy in Public Situations

These guidelines apply when you are in an uncomfortable situation, and/or if you're shy in many public situations.

What to Say
- *"How do you know the hostess?"*
- *"How did you get involved with this organization?"*
- *"How about this weather?"*
- *"Tell me about your job."*

If you need to escape from an overbearing person, or someone you just don't want to be around, or you need a few minutes alone to collect your thoughts, use one of the following phrases;
- *"Excuse me, I need to make a phone call."* (even if you're just calling directory assistance to make sure your phone number has not changed).
- *"Oh, look at the time! Nice talking to you."* (and walk away).
- *"Excuse me . . . "* (and walk away like you're headed somewhere important).

What Not to Say
- Anything negative or critical to someone you do not know.

What to Do
- Give the person you have to talk to a genuine compliment—about her dress, the food, his singing voice, or how well the event is organized.
- Prepare for the event by reading the newspaper, the website of the organization whose event you are attending, etc., so you have something to talk about.
- Pray for confidence; remind yourself that God loves you and you are His child.
- Wear something that makes you feel confident.
- Smile; it's easy to look unhappy if you're uncomfortable.
- Keep something in your hands; a drink, camera, program, magazine, etc. Having something in your hands gives you something to do and will give you a bit of confidence.

Don't . . .
- . . . stand with your arms crossed, or turn away from someone who is talking with you; this appears rude even if you're doing it out of discomfort.

Chapter Two

Love, Marriage, and Children

Many sticky, tricky, uncomfortable situations involve relationships and children.

Expressing Concern about a Relationship/ Potential Spouse

Before you voice concern to a friend about the person she is dating and/or planning to marry, ask yourself; are you being critical of a personality trait or a true character issue? Just because you don't like the fact that someone your friend is dating collects ceramic scorpions, enjoys easy listening music, or wears plaid pants with white shoes, does not mean he or she is not a good match for your friend.

However, a person with negative character traits or very dissimilar morals or values *can* hurt your friend emotionally, spiritually, or physically. If you know first hand that the person your friend is dating has a sexually transmitted disease, criminal record, other children or spouses, an addiction, or another potential harmful character trait, tell your friend; she deserves to know all pertinent facts so she can make an informed decision about the future of the relationship.

If you decide to bring up the subject, reassure your friend that you have her best interests in mind. Then state the facts objectively. Here are a few suggestions for what to say and do.

What to Say
- "He has not held a steady job for three years; I know you hope to have children and stay home with them someday but it will be hard for you to do that if he doesn't have a steady job."
- "Remember, he is obligated to pay child support until the child from his previous relationship is 18 years old."
- "Are you prepared to have the children from his first marriage at your home every other weekend?"
- "I have seen him with his kids from previous relationships; he was very impatient and spanked them frequently. I am worried he will mistreat your children too."
- "She dropped out of school and is living with her parents and not working; do you really think she is ready to take on the responsibilities of being a wife?"
- "Since I live in the same town as your prospective fiancé, I've seen that her parents have interfered with her sisters' marriages and caused many problems by insisting they spend every holiday and birthday with them, excluding the husbands' families completely. How do you feel about them doing that to you?"
- "She has had several arrests just this year related to drugs and drunk driving."
- "He did not finish high school, so it will be very difficult for him to get a job and earn money to buy a home. Are you prepared to be the main bread-winner forever?"
- "I heard him bragging about spending the night with a stripper last weekend."

If your friend becomes engaged and you're concerned about the marriage, state your worries.
- "You've only known him for a few months, and in a month he's going to be deployed overseas for more than a year. Many marriages under these circumstances end in divorce, even if the couple has been married for years. War changes people; please think about these challenges and consider not marrying until he returns and you get to know each other better."
- "I would not be a true friend if I did not tell you why I'm concerned about your getting married to her."

- *"God intends marriage to last forever (Matt. 19:6)—do you see that happening in this case?"*

What Not to Say
- *"You'd be really stupid to marry her."*
- *"She's a jerk—why would you want to even date her?"*
- *"Don't come running to me if it doesn't work out!"*

What to Do
- Pray for guidance to say the right thing, and for your friend to seek God's will.
- Realize that your cautionary comments may cause tension between you and your friend.
- Understand that for some people, dating (or even marrying), unsuitable partners is a pattern. If your friend fits this example, point this out to her, and suggest counseling or talking with a clergy person (for premarital counseling, if they are engaged), in hopes that she can develop healthier relationships.
- Be open to getting to know the person your friend is dating/marrying. Your point of view has more credibility when you do know the person, and perhaps when you do get to know him, you will find your negative impression was not accurate.
- Consider enlisting the help of other close friends or a pastor or priest to talk with your friend about the issues.
- If you are very opposed to the marriage, you might choose to refuse to attend the wedding. However, remember that if the marriage turns out badly, your friend might need you in the future but be reluctant to ask for your help if you cut all ties. Consider maintaining the relationship so your friend feels like she can come to you for help if she needs you in the future.
- Share your feelings and assure your friend of your support by saying something like; *"I do not approve of your dating/marrying this person, but I will always be available if you need me!"*

Don't . . .
- . . . cut off all ties with the person.

- ... worry more about your friend's relationship than your friend is.
- ... gossip about the situation.

Marriage Problems and Divorce

When Someone is Having Marriage Problems
A person who is having marriage problems needs support, friendship, and encouragement. This stressful time can be very lonely, and the person having the problems will be thankful for having someone to trust, talk to, and depend on.

What to Say
- *"I'm sorry to hear the two of you are having problems."*
- *"Do you want to tell me about it?"*
- *"People have been asking me what is going on between you and Chris. What do you want me to tell them?"*
- *"I've been in the same situation and my husband and I worked it out. Do you want me to tell you about it?"*
- *"How are the kids?"*
- *"How are you doing?"*
- *"It is OK to be mad/sad/upset at what is happening ... and to have mixed feelings about it all."*
- *"It is OK to cry."*
- *"You're in my thoughts and prayers."*
- *"This must be a very hard time for you."*
- If you are a close friend, say, *"God wants marriages to last—have you talked with your pastor/priest/rabbi about these problems?"* (Do not place undue pressure on the person to remain married unless you know all the details. Remaining married may not be an option.)
- *"Have the two of you thought about seeing a counselor?"* If so, suggest a counselor or offer to ask other friends for a recommendation.

What Not to Say
- *"All men are horrible/all women are horrible."*
- *"You would be better off without her."*
- *"He is such a jerk!"*
- *"I knew she was trouble from the day you got married!"*

What to Do
- Pray for your friends to reconcile, if that is God's will
- Reassure your friend that she is not alone, and that you will continue to be a friend.
- Let the person vent, cry, panic; listen and do not cut her off no matter what emotions or feelings she is expressing.
- If your friend shares details, be nonjudgmental. Offer remarks like, *"That's a tough situation!" "WOW—I bet your were surprised to find that out!"* or *"What a shock!"*
- Offer a hug.
- Offer to go with your friend to an appointment with a counselor, pastor, or lawyer.
- Offer to take care of the kids during counseling appointments, meetings with the lawyer, or just to give the couple time alone together.
- Invite your friend to go with you to a movie or out for coffee, to help her get her mind off her troubles temporarily.

Don't . . .
- . . . join in if the person criticizes his or her spouse. It's OK to listen, but don't add your perceptions of the spouse's shortcomings.
- . . . talk about the marriage problems every time you see or talk to the person. It's OK if she brings it up, but she might need a break and want to talk about something else.
- . . . be pushy about your religious beliefs regarding marriage. It's OK to mention God's plan for marriage, but remember that circumstances of the marriage (abuse, adultery, addictions) could make divorce the only option.
- . . . gossip about the marriage or problems associated with it.

When Friends Divorce

What to Say
- *"You are in my thoughts and prayers as you go through this hard time."*
- *"I'm so sorry this happened!"*
- *"How are you doing?"*
- If one friend asks you to not be friends with his or her ex, say, *"I'm not going to choose, but I won't talk about the situation with your ex."*
- If one spouse is clearly at fault, it's OK to recognize that and say to the other, *"What he did was very wrong. I'm so sorry it had to happen to you! I'll be here for you and do whatever I can to help you through this time."*

What Not to Say
- *"He was such a jerk. You're better off now."*
- *"Don't worry, you'll find someone else in no time."*
- *"I'm surprised you stayed married as long as you did."*
- *"You should have divorced her the first time she cheated on you."*
- *"God will punish you for divorcing. You can't get married again."* (Most Christians believe there are some circumstance in which divorce is allowed.)

What to Do
- Pray for God's will to be done by your friends, and for God to guide your actions.
- If you are hosting a party or other get-together and inviting both ex-spouses, tell them both the other will be there and let them choose if they will attend or not.
- If one of the spouses is clearly at fault in the divorce, or makes the process difficult, you will probably not want to remain friends with him or her. You might want to just let the friendship fade away, or you might want to say something like, *"I just don't agree with what you've done and want to support (the*

other person's name) in this matter. Perhaps we can pick up our friendship at a later time."

Don't . . .
- . . . surprise the ex's by inviting them both to an event.
- . . . talk about one ex-spouse to the other.
- . . . encourage your friend to date before she is ready.
- . . . focus just on the divorce; it's OK to talk about it if she brings it up, but talk about other things if she steers the conversation away from the divorce.

Holidays and Wedding Anniversaries During Marriage Problems or After Divorce

Holidays (including their wedding anniversary), will probably bring conflicting emotions to people who are having marriage problems or are divorced. Sadness about the relationship ending might be mixed with relief if it was an abusive relationship or there were long-term problems. Good memories of holidays—even if they were few and far between—and the necessity of starting new traditions, can add to the mix of feelings about the day.

What to Say
- *"How are you spending the holiday next week?"*
- *"Do you want some company?"*
- *"Where are the kids spending the holiday?"*
- *"You are certainly invited to spend the day with us!"* If the person turns down the invitation and plans to spend the day alone, add, *"You are welcome at our house, even at the last minute."*

The anniversary of their marriage is significant and will be remembered, even if the couple is having problems or is divorced.
- *"I know your wedding anniversary is coming up; how do you feel about it?"* Accept her feelings, whether she is happy, sad, or ambivalent about the date.
- *"Would you like some company tomorrow?"* (the date of the anniversary).
- *"Would you like to go with me to a movie that night?"*

- *"I know this is your anniversary, and know it's been a difficult year. I'm thinking of you."*
- *"Would you like to go out this afternoon?"* (Don't do this as a celebration, but as a time to get away and talk if she wants to.)

What Not to Say
- *"Just don't think about it."*
- *"Forget all the years you had together; they mean nothing."*
- *"It's a good thing that you're not married anymore."*

What to Do
- Let your friend guide the conversation to, or away from, talking about the significance of the date.
- Call the person on the holiday or anniversary and invite him to your home or offer to go out with him to supper or a movie.
- Let your friend's mood guide your actions; if she's cheerful, don't try to make her sad. If she's sad, accept and acknowledge her feelings.
- Accept how your friend chooses to spend the day.

Don't . . .
- . . . try to ignore the date; your friend will remember the significance.
- . . . focus on the significance of the date if your friend clearly wants to talk about something else.

If Your Marriage is in Trouble or You are Getting a Divorce
Ask for the support and friendship you need to work through this tough time. How much information you want to share with others, about your problems, is up to you.

What to Say
- *"We are having some marriage problems right now, and I need someone to talk to. Do you have time?"*
- *"We're having some problems but working through them."*
- *Things are going a bit better."*

- *"Thanks for your concern; we're working on straightening things out but I'm really not comfortable talking about it right now."*
- *"We were not able to work through our problems and unfortunately are divorcing."*
- *"I don't want to talk about it right now, but will you please keep us in your prayers?"*

What Not to Say
- *"Quit asking questions!"* (Say this in a nicer way.)

What to Do
- Pray for God's guidance as to what you should do, and from whom you should seek support.
- Thank people for their support.
- Ask for favors that you need—watching the kids while you are at marriage counseling, etc.
- Be very careful about sharing the details of your problems with friends or acquaintances.

Don't . . .
- . . . share all the details of your marriage problems with everyone. At a later date you might be uncomfortable with many people knowing intimate details, especially if you and your spouse are able to work out your problems.

Fertility Problems

When Someone is Having Problems
Approximately 10% of couples of childbearing age who wish to have children are not able to. Many choose to undergo medical treatments in an attempt to become pregnant. Some people may be comfortable sharing the details of their struggles with you, while others may not. If a friend confides that she's having fertility problems, here's how you can help.

What to Say
- *"I'm sorry you're having problems!"*
- *"We had trouble conceiving a baby, too. It was a very difficult time in my life."* (Don't go into details about what you went through unless she asks; the conversation is not about you!)
- *"My husband/wife and I had fertility problems and made it through them . . . If you'd like to hear how we coped with it all, please let us know."*
- *"May I ask what you've been trying? If you'd rather not talk about it I understand."*
- *"I hope whatever you're trying goes well. We will be thinking of/praying for you."*
- *"I'll pray for God's peace and continued direction in your lives."*
- *"Whatever happens is all in God's plan . . . "*

In a few months, or after a test or procedure she's told you about, it's OK to ask:
- *"You were telling me a bit about your attempts at having a baby, a few months ago. How are things going?"*
- *"How did the procedure/test go?"*
- *"What did the test results show?"*

What Not to Say
- *"If you just relax, you'll get pregnant."*
- *"Do you not like kids?"*
- *"Can't you try harder?"*
- *"You're lucky not to have kids these days."*
- *"You can have my kids!"*
- *"You won't miss what you never had."*
- *"You might not have been a good parent anyway."*
- *"I just know God will give you your miracle baby!"* (no, you do not know that!).
- *"You're not missing anything; kids cost too much and take too much time."*
- *"I guess you waited too long to try to have kids."*
- *"You're so lucky you've never had to suffer through pregnancy."*
- *"Having step kids is exactly the same as having your own."*

- "Just accept God's will and move on. You've been trying long enough."
- "Have you thought about adoption?" (Adoption is a well-known option that every couple having fertility problems has thought about.)
- "Have you tried . . . " Unless you are a doctor or researcher who has just discovered a new technique, they've most likely tried, or are aware of, everything there is to try!
- "Studies show marriages are happier if you don't have kids, anyway."
- "God must not want you to have children."

Snappy Comebacks to some thoughtless comments:

<u>Thoughtless Comment:</u>
"You're so lucky not to have kids these days!"

<u>Snappy Comeback:</u>
"So are you cursed because you have kids?"
"Do your kids know you say that?"

<u>Thoughtless Comment:</u>
"Can't you try harder?"

<u>Snappy Comeback:</u>
"If we tried any harder, our bed would fall apart!"

<u>Thoughtless Comment:</u>
"You can have my kids."

<u>Snappy Comeback:</u>
"Do your kids know you feel that way?"
"Draw up the adoption papers!"

What to Do
- Pray for your friends to accept God's will in their attempt to have children.
- Realize that a couple is a family; children are not required to make a family.
- Be sensitive to the fact that the person might not want to talk about fertility problems or treatments, especially if things are not going well. It's OK to ask how things are going, but if he or she does not seem to want to talk about it, don't push.
- Invite your friend for a girl's night out, without kids and without mention of children.
- Call to see how your friend is doing, especially if you know it's a day she had tests, a procedure, or received test results.
- When meeting someone for the first time, instead of asking, *"Do you have children?"* ask, *"Do you have family in the area?"* (Asking about children first may seem to imply that is the most important thing about the person.)

Don't . . .
- . . . send maternity clothes, baby supplies or baby furniture 'for later.'
- . . . stop calling after you have children; your friend still needs your friendship. If she calls when you are busy with your children, offer to call back later so you can talk without being interrupted.

Announcing a Pregnancy, or Baby Shower

Before you make an announcement to a group of people about a pregnancy or baby shower (your own or someone else's), be aware of the fact that someone you are announcing it to could be struggling with infertility. This does not mean you should not share the good news, just be sensitive to reactions of people when they hear it. If you know, or find out later, that someone is struggling with fertility issues, here are some suggestions for how to handle the situation.

What to Say
- *"I realize you're trying very hard to get pregnant. Does it bother you to hear me talk about my pregnancy? If so, I'll try not to do it when you're around."*
- *"I know you have been trying to have a baby (or were never able to). Since we're friends, I wanted to tell you in private that I am pregnant."*
- *"I didn't know you were having trouble conceiving. I hope the news of my pregnancy wasn't hard for you to hear! If it was, I apologize; I certainly didn't mean to cause you pain."*
- *"We are giving a baby shower for Rachel next week. I know it's a difficult time for you as you've been trying to get pregnant, so I wanted to tell you in private about the shower. We'd love for you to be there, but if you don't want to attend, I understand."*

What Not to Say
- *"You are selfish if you're not happy for me/don't attend the shower."*
- In front of other people, *"Since you're having problems, I bet you don't want to come."*

What to Do
- Realize that some people who are struggling with fertility issues might find the subjects of pregnancy and babies very painful. If you notice a friend, co-worker, or family member tearing up or leaving the room when the conversation turns to pregnancy or children, try not to discuss the subject when that person is present.
- On the other hand, if the person who is struggling with fertility issues assures you that she does *not* mind talk of pregnancy or babies, don't be afraid to include her in those conversations.
- Realize that people of 'grandparent' age, who were not able to have children, may be having similar feelings when their friends are having grandchildren.

Don't . . .
- . . . automatically send ultrasound pictures (via mail or e-mail) to everyone on your list; be selective, especially if you know someone on your list is struggling with fertility issues.
- . . . push someone who is having fertility problems to attend a baby shower if she has turned down the invitation.
- . . . push someone you know is struggling with pregnancy issues to look at ultrasound pictures, listen to the details regarding your pregnancy, or attend a baby shower.
- . . . push someone who was unable to have children, to look at pictures of your grandchildren.

If You are Having Fertility Problems

Some people are comfortable sharing every detail of their struggle to have a child. Other people are not. You are *not* obligated to share any details you do not want to! Here are some responses to comments or questions.

What to Say
- *"That's a very personal question!"*
- *"I really don't want to talk about it."*
- *"We've been having problems conceiving, but we're trying."*
- *"I'm going to have a procedure next week."*
- *"I've had several miscarriages and we're trying to figure out why."*
- *"We're having trouble getting pregnant and would appreciate your prayers."*
- With a smile; *"You can ask two questions—that's the weekly limit."*
- If you are getting too many questions about fertility treatments, say (with a smile), *"You're welcome to come to our next appointment; he's going to give a sperm sample and the doctor is going to check my endometrium."* Most people will get the point—that they're asking too many questions.
- If you want to talk to someone who had trouble conceiving, just ask! Say something like, *"I know you had trouble conceiving a*

baby. We're going through that now. Do you mind talking about it?"

If asked when you are going to have children:
- *"When it's the perfect time for us."*
- *"We're having some problems, but working with good doctors."*
- *"It's taking longer than we thought . . . But we're trying!"*
- *"You'll be one of the first to know."*
- *"I'll let you know when we find out."*

What Not to Say
- *"Quit bugging me about it!" "Don't ask any more questions!"* (try to answer more politely).
- *"I can't believe you're so rude to talk about your pregnancy when I'm around. You should know I'm having problems getting pregnant."*

What to Do
- React calmly to questions, at least the first time you are asked; if you are asked frequently by the same person, it's OK to show your emotions and ask the person firmly not to talk about it.

Don't . . .
- . . . feel obligated to talk about anything you don't want to.
- . . . give a harsh answer, unless the same person has asked many times despite your request for him not to.

If You are Having Fertility Problems and Someone Else Becomes Pregnant

If you are having difficulty becoming pregnant, you might find it hard to be happy to be around anyone who is pregnant. Share their happiness to the extent you can, but do not feel guilty if you choose not to look at ultrasound pictures or take part in conversations about pregnancy or attend baby showers.

What to Say
- *"I'm so happy for you that you are having a baby! However, we have been struggling with getting/staying pregnant, and it's hard for me to hear about someone else's success. I wish you every happiness, but I just can't talk about it today."*
- *"Because I can't have children, it's difficult for me to attend baby showers. But I hope you have a great time!"*
- *"I'm happy for you, but it's hard for me to look at ultrasound pictures when I know I'll never get pregnant. Please don't push me to look at them."*
- If you sense someone is uncomfortable talking about their pregnancy when you are present, but you share her joy and don't mind hearing the details, reassure her; *"I'm disappointed that I cannot have children, but I'm so happy for you, and glad to hear all the details."*

What Not to Say
- *"How can you be celebrating when other people can't have children?"*

What to Do
- Pray for God to help you to have peace with your situation.
- Quietly leave the room if you don't want to listen to conversations about pregnancy or children.
- Politely decline invitations to baby showers if you're not comfortable attending.

Don't . . .
- . . . take receiving invitations to baby showers, even if you have explained that you will not attend, as anything but a friendly gesture. Even if the person putting on the shower knows you will not attend, she probably wants you to feel included and welcome to come if you change your mind. It's OK to politely decline invitations.
- . . . feel obligated to stay in the room where pregnancy or children are being discussed, if you are not comfortable doing so.

Adoption

When Friends Choose to Adopt

What to Say
- "*Congratulations!*"
- "*What do you know about the child/baby?*" (if the parents have not received the baby yet)
- If the baby has similar eye or hair coloring as the parents, "*She looks like you!*"
- "*The baby is blessed to have you for her parents.*"
- "*Your family is so blessed to have him!*"

What Not to Say
- "*Don't you want to have 'real' children?*"
- "*You won't love her as much as you love your 'real' kids.*"
- "*She doesn't look like any of you!*"
- "*What if the birth mother wants him back?*"
- "*What are you going to do when he wants to meet his 'real' parents?*"

What to Do
- Frequently ask how things are progressing and how 'waiting' is going; the process of adoption can take a long time.
- Keep the adoptive parents and family in your prayers.
- Be positive and accepting of the decision to adopt, even if it's not something you would have chosen.
- Accept the child as a member of the family.
- Be sensitive about using terms like 'natural parents,' 'biological parents,' 'gave up,' etc. Ask the parents which terms they prefer, or listen to and use the terms they do.

Don't . . .
- . . . tell any negative stories about adoption, but if something seems out of place—they're not working with a lawyer, for example—it's OK to question what they're doing and encourage them to consult a lawyer.

- ... criticize choices the parents have made—if the adopted child's birth parents will have contact with the child, when and how the child will be told he or she is adopted, and so on. It's OK to offer your opinion if you're asked.
- ... ask for details concerning the child's birth or parents. That is private information.

If Adoption Plans Fall Through

What to Say
- *"I'm so sorry it didn't work out!"*
- *"I'm here for you no matter what."*
- *"You and your family are in my thoughts and prayers."*
- *"I'll be glad to watch your children so you can get out of the house or just have some time to yourself."*
- *"If you want to talk about it, I'm a good listener."*

What Not to Say
- *"Those arrangements never work."*
- *"You're just not meant to have children."*
- *"At least you have your other kids!"* (Children are not interchangeable!)
- *"That baby wasn't yours anyway." "It's not like you lost your baby."* (The baby did belong to the parents, even if just for a short time and even if the parents did not ever get to see the baby.)
- *"It's better if the baby is with the birth mother—that's the natural way."*
- *"It probably wouldn't have worked out anyway."*
- *"Sue the agency!"* (The parents don't want money, they want their baby!)

What to Do
- Pray for the family. Pray for their peace, and that they will accept God's will for them.
- Call your friend frequently.
- Invite your friend out for lunch or to a movie.

- Support the family in their continued quest for a baby, whatever course they choose.

Don't . . .
- . . . ask for baby supplies.
- . . . discourage them from attempting adoption again.

When You've Adopted

If people make negative comments about your choice to adopt, here are some suggestions of how to reply;

What to Say
- "That was a thoughtless comment . . ."
- "We're so blessed that God has brought this child into our family!"
- "We are her 'real' parents. She is our 'real' child."

f you are asked about issues like contact with the adopted child's birth parents, if, how and when you will tell the child he or she is adopted, and so on, say;
- "We'll resolve those issues at the right time, in a way that is right for our family."
- "We have thought very hard to make the right decision for our family."

What Not to Say
- "That's none of your business." (Say this in a nicer way.)

What to Do
- Pray for the right response to difficult questions or comments.
- Stay calm even when people make thoughtless comments or ask intrusive questions.
- Present the facts objectively and calmly.
- Educate people about issues related to adoption.

Don't . . .
- . . . be rude.

Parents and Their Children

Other Children and Your Child

In every young child's life there seems to be, on occasion, a child who hits, kicks or bites; doesn't share; screams or spits, and generally makes it difficult for your child to enjoy his company. The situation is made worse if the other child's parents do not make their child behave in a socially acceptable manner. Here are some tactful ways to try to remedy the situation.

What to Say
- To the parent; *"My child is a bit intimidated by your child's yelling and screaming while they are playing. Could you talk with him about that before he comes over?"*
- To the child (in front of the parent if possible); *"We have a new rule at our house; no calling names. Anyone who does has to sit in the time-out chair. This includes moms, dads, and visitors."*
- To the parent: *"I'm working hard to teach our children about sharing. Is Clyde used to sharing? I'll talk to him about it when he's here."*
- If the situation is not improving, say to the parent, *"Our children just don't seem to be enjoying each other's company lately. Let's take a break from play-dates for awhile. I'm sure it's just a stage and they'll enjoy playing together again soon."*

What Not to Say
- *"You're just not disciplining your child like you should be. If you were, he wouldn't be acting this way."*
- *"Your kid is a brat and terrorizes other kids."*

What to Do
- If the issues causing you discomfort are differences in parenting style (how the parents discipline their child, for example), be careful not to sound judgmental.
- Remember that what you say or do could potentially damage your relationship with the child's parents and your child's friendship.

- If you feel the friendship is not healthy for your child, or your child no longer wants to spend time with the child, gently cut off play-dates. Don't invite the child over for play-dates, and politely decline play-date invitations. If you do this several times, the friendship will probably gradually fade out. If the invitations continue, you might want to say something like, *"This summer will be very busy for us; we won't have time for play-dates." "We've been so busy lately, we've decided to just concentrate on family things for awhile. I'll let you know when we're ready for play-dates again."*
- If the offending child's home life is chaotic, contact with your family might be the only stability in the child's life. Keep this fact in mind when you consider cutting off play-dates.

Don't...
- ...overreact to minor skirmishes or disagreements between children.

Following Your House Rules

Make your household rules—about snacks, language, running in the house, phone use, acceptable movies, TV shows, and videos, whether shoes should be on or off when kids are in the house, and so on—clear to visiting child(ren) and parents (depending on the age of the kids) before any play-date.

What to Say
- *"When we invite someone for the first play date, I always explain the rules . . . "*
- *"Every family has different rules; here are ours . . . "*
- *"Let's go over the rules, just to make sure everyone follows them and we have a great time today!"*
- *"We have a few new rules since you were here last week . . . "*

What Not to Say
- *"Follow our rules, or else!"*
- *"I don't care what the rules are at your house, here are ours."*

What to Do
- Mention relevant rules and family routines when you make the play-date; *"We play outside a lot, so be sure to bring a hat and mittens." "We have new carpet, so everyone takes their shoes off when they're in the house. Bring slippers if your feet get cold!"*
- Review the rules with younger children (including your child) at the beginning of each play date and when the rules change.
- Consider posting the rules on the refrigerator or other public spot.
- When your children are old enough, let them explain the rules to their friends and give them the responsibility for making sure they're followed (tell them to come to you if a friend won't follow the rules).
- Enforce the rules equally with your children and the guests.
- Make sure your rules are clear; they might be very different from the rules at the visitor's home.
- Encourage your children to follow the rules at their friends' homes.

Don't . . .
- . . . make exceptions to the rules or kids will take advantage of you.
- . . . be intimidated to change or bend the rules if kids complain that your rules are 'different' or 'strict.'

If a Child Won't Follow the Rules
It is reasonable to expect children visiting your home to follow your rules. Doing so teaches them a very valuable lesson about rules and respect.

What to Say
- *"It's OK to have fun, but you still have to follow the rules. No running in the house!"*
- *"Remember the rules—no slamming doors! If I hear the door slam again, you'll have to stop playing that game."*
- *"When you are at our house, I expect you to follow our rules. If you choose not to, here's what happens to our kids; you will have the same consequence if you continue what you are doing."*

What Not to Say
- *"Just because your parents let you get away with anything doesn't mean we will at our house."*

What to Do
- Follow through with consequences in a kind, calm, matter-of-fact way.
- If the visiting child's behavior is very disrupting, call the parents to come and pick the child up. Say something like, *"Things just are not going well; Jake is screaming and swearing and the kids are not getting along. We need to end the play-date early and try again another day. Can you come and pick him up?"*
- If a child breaks the rules and you have to carry out a consequence, explain your actions to the parents in a calm, non-judgmental way: *"Terry got a bit overexcited today and was running around and slamming the doors. One of our house rules is no running in the house, and no slamming doors. I was afraid someone was going to get hurt, so I had him sit down for a few minutes to calm down."*

Don't . . .
- . . . apologize for your rules.
- . . . ever spank anyone else's child; it is just not your place and could be a legal risk.
- . . . back down and bend or ignore your own rules.

If You are Uncomfortable with the Environment of Your Child's Friend's Home

Perhaps you are not comfortable letting your child play at a certain friend's home because supervision of the children is lax, the parents smoke or drink excessively, you suspect there are illegal drugs being used in the home, or there are other adults present and you are not comfortable with these adults being around your child. Whatever the reason, trust your instincts and do not let your child go to that house if you are not comfortable with the environment. Here are some things you can say and do if you're in this tricky situation.

What to Say
- *"My child is going through a phase where he prefers to play at home. Can we have play-dates here for awhile?"*
- *"He's happier at home lately so I'd rather have him here."*
- *"We're potty training, and that is easier to do at our home."*
- *"I'm working on a project at home. If we have the play-date here, I can work on my project while the kids are playing."*
- If the parent continues to issue invitations, be honest, but in a gentle way; *"I don't want to expose my child to secondhand smoke, and at our house he is not." "I'm uncomfortable having adult non-family members like your boyfriend, present where my daughter is. Maybe I'm overly-cautious, but it's just the way I am." "I just love having the kids play at my house—they're so fun to have around!" "I don't feel comfortable if my child is in a home where guns are present, even if they are locked up." "My child has a lot of allergies and I can better protect him from coming in contact with them, at home."*

What Not to Say
- *"Your family is a bad influence with your poor values."*
- *"I just don't like your lifestyle."* (Say this in a nicer way!)

What to Do
- Pray about what to do to keep your child safe.
- If your child is old enough to understand, explain the reasons you are reluctant to let him go to a friend's home. Allow him to invite his friend to your home.

Don't . . .
- . . . feel intimidated into letting your child go because the friend keeps inviting him.

Kids Behaving Badly

If Someone's Kids are Behaving Badly
Should you tell someone her kids are doing something you know she, as a parent, would not approve of? Before you pass on any information about her child, be sure the action or behavior you're reporting is something that could harm the child (or another person), or is something you *know* the parents would not approve of. While you might not let your kids wear shorts if it is below 60 degrees outside, some parents let their kids wear shorts regardless of the temperature. Another example: In some families, using certain words might be acceptable, even if they are not words you allow used in your home. If you report something like this to parents and it is within their family rules, you risk sounding judgmental.

If the child is doing something that is against the law—stealing, drinking alcohol, smoking—or putting himself or others in danger by posting her home address on an Internet chat site or talking about bringing a gun to school, you have an obligation to tell his or her parents, and the proper authorities, if necessary.

Do not pass on any information about a child's behavior or actions unless you actually saw the event happen or know the information is accurate. The parent's first reaction might be to become angry with you; stay calm, reassure the parent of your intentions to protect the child, and offer to help the parent deal with the problem. Here are several ways to approach this difficult situation.

What to Say
- "Since teens have such a high rate of accidents anyway, I wanted to tell you that I saw Seymore driving well above the speed limit the other day, and he was not wearing his seatbelt."
- "I would want this information passed on to me if it was one of my children, so I wanted to let you know that I saw Carlie smoking with a group of kids outside of the school yesterday."
- "My mother saw Dexter at the mall yesterday during school hours; she knew it was him because he was wearing his letter jacket with his name on it."

- *"My kids came home very upset after Leslie told them she was going to bring beer and a gun to school in her backpack tomorrow."*
- *"My children were checking out your daughter's online profile yesterday—there are some very suggestive photos on it, along with her cell phone number."*

What Not to Say
- *"I don't know if it's actually true but you need to know that I heard that . . ."*
- *"Your kid is going to get into big trouble if you don't start paying attention . . ."*

What to Do
- Pray for the wisdom to handle the situation in a way that will protect the child.
- Be kind, pleasant, and non-judgmental when you talk to the parents about their child. Remind them that you told them in order to help their child.
- Offer to give parents the phone number of a counselor, name of a helpful book, information about group meetings, or other resources as applicable to the situation, without being pushy.
- Realize that giving the parents this information could cause tension in your friendship. Remember that you're doing it for the safety and well-being of their child and others.

Don't . . .
- . . . pass on second, or third, or fourth hand information.

If Someone Else's Kids are Having Problems

It's a difficult time for a friend if her child is in trouble. Whether the problem is minor (problems in school or with a bad attitude), or more serious (stealing, using drugs, being involved with a gang), parents will appreciate your support and encouragement.

What to Say
- *"You are all in our prayers."*
- *"It must be difficult to have this going on in your life."*
- *"I know you taught her different than that; sometimes as parents we just can't prevent things like this."*
- *"Our child went through a stage where he didn't want to go to church and turned away from God; it only lasted a few months but seemed like much longer. Hang in there! I'm here if you want to talk about it."*
- *"How are things with Colleen going?"*
- *"When my kids were doing that, I . . ."*
- *"A book that really helped us was . . ."*
- *"You are doing the right thing, even though it is difficult."*
- *"I have the name of a counselor who is good with children of that age. Would you like the name and number?"*
- *"God gives our children free will to make their own decisions, no matter what we've taught them."*
- *"Your work as a parent was* not *in vain."*
- *"Your children have made a lot of good choices; this is just one negative one."*
- *"Hang in there . . . this too shall pass."*

What Not to Say
- *"Here's what you need to do."*
- *"You better do something or he'll turn into an axe murderer!"*
- *"He's that way because . . ."*
- *"Well that won't help!"* (when said as a reply to what the parents are trying to do to help the child).

What to Do
- Pray for God to guide the parents to do the right thing for their child.
- Call or e-mail to offer encouragement.
- Listen without judgment; allow the parent to express his or her feelings/emotions, and accept his or her feelings of anger, sadness, disappointment, fear, and so on.
- Offer to go with the person to seek information, talk with a lawyer, etc.

- Take younger kids in the family to the movies or park or out to eat, to give the parents some time alone together or with the child who is having problems.

Don't . . .
- . . . criticize what the parents are doing (or not doing).
- . . . spread information you don't know is true.

If Your Kid is in Trouble

What to Say
- *"We're disappointed at the path he's taking, but we still love him."*
- *"That's not how we brought him up, but he's still our child."*
- *"We're doing everything we can to help."*
- *"We're keeping the details to ourselves; we're doing everything we need to."*
- *"We are respecting our daughter's privacy in this; please pray for her to make good decisions."*
- *"Please keep our family in your prayers."*

What Not to Say
- *"Don't ask about it!"* (Be polite about requesting your privacy.)

What to Do
- Pray for guidance to do what is best for your child.
- Ask parents who have been through troubles with their children, for help.

Don't . . .
- . . . share any details you're not comfortable sharing.

Chapter 3

Difficult People

We all qualify for the title of "difficult person," at least occasionally, but some people take the role to an extreme. Use the less dramatic comments below to help a person back to a more realistic outlook during a bad day. Use the more biting, sarcastic comments carefully; sometimes a reply of this nature is needed to snap a person back to reality or enable him to see how he's really coming across. If you make your remarks with a smile, and in a neutral tone of voice, it will take away the sting while getting your point across.

However you answer, do so with respect and Godly love. Remember that we all have eccentricities and quirks that annoy others, and He loves us despite these.
Ask God to give you a 'gentle tongue' as in Proverbs15:4, so His love shows through you, when you respond to difficult people.

<u>Inappropriate, Rude, Critical, or Obnoxious Questions or Comments</u>

When people make an inappropriate comment, they usually don't mean harm, they just don't realize the rudeness of what they said or asked. However, some people consistently go too far with their improper comments and questions.

Consider the circumstances before you make your reply. If the comment comes from a stranger who just left her manners at home, answer with a smile. On the other hand, if the person who made the remark has a history of asking overly-personal questions or making hurtful comments, you might offer a more biting answer. Whatever your approach, do it in a spirit of Christian love and grace.

What To Say
- With a disbelieving expression, ask, *"What did you just say?"* (Sometimes if the person repeats the comment, he or she will realize how inappropriate it was.)
- *"Wow! What a question! There is no right answer to that one!"*
- *"That's kind of an inappropriate thing to say . . . "*
- *"That is something I'm not going to talk about."*
- *"I don't discuss that with anyone but my family."*

See the Appendix of this book for more comebacks to specific comments or questions.

What Not to Say
- *"You are a horrible person for asking such snoopy questions all the time. I don't ever want to hear you do that again."*
- *"Obviously your mother didn't teach you any manners!"*

What to Do
- Try silence, and an *"I-can't-believe-you-just-said-that!"* shocked look, with your eyes wide, mouth open, and eyebrows raised; perhaps the person will realize how inappropriate the question/comment was, and change the subject.
- Remain pleasant and kind; you can make your point while responding with grace.
- Change the subject without acknowledging the comment or question.
- Let the tone and inflections in your voice speak as much as your words.

Don't . . .
- . . . respond in kind by returning an insult or asking an equally inappropriate question.
- . . . answer a rude or inappropriate question you don't want to.

The Person Who Talks and Talks and Talks . . .

This section does not apply to someone who is going through a difficult time and needs to talk about it, but to people who constantly talk (sometimes about nothing significant), never pausing for a breath or comment, despite subtle (or not so subtle!) signals from you.

A person who talks constantly (whether in person or on the phone) might be lonely and craving contact; if you suspect this is the case, be compassionate and listen for at least a few minutes. However, if the person has a habit of going on and on (and on and on), and you simply must get back to whatever you were doing (whether at home, your place of employment, while you're shopping or at the gym), don't allow yourself to be held captive.

What to Say
- *"It was great to talk to you, but I need to get back to shopping/ working out/cleaning."*
- *"How nice you called! I just have 10 minutes and have to get back to work . . . how have you been?"*
- When you're ready to get off the phone, politely say, *"It was great to talk to you, but I need to go. Good bye!"*
- If the person is talking to you during a meeting, *"I want to pay attention to this, so let's talk later."*
- *"I'm working on this project and don't want to get distracted. Can we talk later?"*
- *"I really have to get back to work now! Thanks for calling/stopping by."*
- *"I need quiet to concentrate on this; I'll stop by your office or call you later if I have time. Sorry to kick you out, but I have to get it done!"*

What Not to Say
- *"Wow, please, tell me more!"*
- *"That's so interesting!"*
- *"You talk too much; I have work to do!"* (Be kind.)

What to Do
- Answer kindly, even if you are impatient or frustrated.
- If your work requires concentration, use one of the "What to Say" phrases above and continue what you were doing, even if the person continues to talk.
- Even if your work doesn't require your undivided concentration, consider continuing what you were doing and let the person talk.
- After you've used one of the "What to Say" phrases above, immediately leave the area or go back to your work, so the conversation doesn't get started again.
- If you see the person coming, meet her at the door of your home or office. Talk for the amount of time you have available, then excuse yourself, closing the door behind you.

Don't . . .
- . . . allow yourself to be held captive; it's OK to politely but firmly disengage from the situation.
- . . . maintain eye contact, nod your head, or encourage the person to say anything more.

The Drama Queen or King

You know the personality; every out-of-the-ordinary occurrence is a crisis. A minor health complaint requires visits to the doctor and perhaps a specialist. A perceived snub by someone necessitates talking about it all day, complete with tears. Even world events and national or global issues (the weather, homelessness) can cause this person distress well out of proportion with reality. Nothing can be 'let go'; everything is personal in some way and must be discussed in great detail, often complete with tears.

These people can be exhausting to keep up with! Your goal is to help the person see how overly-dramatic he or she is being, but in a way that does not hurt his or her feelings or irreparably damage your relationship.

What to Say
- *"Wow, that was quite a performance! Are you ready to talk about it calmly, now?"*
- *"Tell me more, tell me more!"* (in a breathless, lightheartedly, sarcastic way).
- *"Since I don't have millions of dollars to donate, and can't go over personally to save them, I'm going to leave the plight of the horny toads in South Africa in God's hands."*
- *"I can tell this is all very upsetting to you . . . Let's get together to talk about it when I have a few minutes to talk about it."* (Sometimes just talking about something relieves some of the stress that leads to drama king or queen performances.)
- *"What can we do about it?"* (depending on the answer, encourage the person to take action or realize that he cannot do anything about this issue).

What Not to Say
- *"Tell me more!"* (if you say it seriously).
- *"Don't be ridiculous."*
- *"What is wrong with you?"*
- *"Why should I care?"* (The person may tell you, in great detail, why you should care!)

What to Do
- Pray for God's guidance to deal with the situation in a way that shows His love.
- Explain your point of view about the issue, objectively.
- Point out the facts about the issue objectively. Perhaps the person will realize that it's not the crisis he or she is making it out to be.
- Try to redirect the conversation to an area that is less emotional, like work, family, or the weather.

- Distance yourself from the person if he/she is taking too much of your time and energy. This is not an easy thing to do, but may be the best solution.
- See the positive aspects of the person beyond his actions.

Don't . . .
- . . . react to the performance; calmly say, *"We've already discussed that,"* and then change the subject.
- . . . dismiss the person; work instead to decrease his behavior.
- . . . get caught up in a discussion if the person is clearly unwilling to consider another point of view; a discussion will only prolong the drama or allow the person to argue his or her position further.

A Person Who is Negative About Everything

This person could find something bad about winning the lottery, not to mention everyday events and good news—or news you thought was good until you talked to her!

What to Say
- *"Think positively!"*
- *"Look at the bright side . . ."*
- *"I've decided to try to look at the positive side of every event; would you like to join me?"*
- *"This is the day that the Lord has made! Let us rejoice and be glad in it!"* (Ps. 118:24)

What Not to Say
- *"Don't be such a negative crab all the time."*
- *"Nothing good is ever going to happen to you."*
- *"You're right, everything is terrible and bad and negative."*

What to Do
- Continue to be positive and try to influence the person to be positive.
- Be kind in what you say and do.
- Consider pulling away from the person if his negativity begins to affect your attitude and outlook.

Don't . . .
- . . . get dragged down by the person's negativity.
- . . . dismiss the person, just his negative attribute.

If Someone is Always Critical of Others

People who are always critical are often unhappy in their own lives, and pointing out the faults of others is a manifestation of their own dissatisfaction. Constant criticism can also be a cover for insecurities and the fear that the critic's own faults will be discovered, maybe because he has been severely criticized by others in the past. Or perhaps the person has been critical of people and things throughout his life, and it's natural for him to find fault in every situation. Insights to reasons behind the criticism can help you respond in a compassionate manner.

What to Say
- "I make it my goal to find something positive in every situation."
- "I've made a goal not to say anything negative about anyone."
- "Remember, no one is perfect."
- "Those are pretty critical things to say about someone who I know is trying very hard to do a good job."

When the person is critical of you:
- "OUCH! That remark hurt . . ."
- "I get discouraged when you are so critical of everything I do."
- "I worked very hard on that and it is hurtful when you criticize what I've done."

- *"Your critical remarks hurt me."*
- *"I am not going to listen to your unfair criticisms."*

What Not to Say
- *"You're such a crab all the time!"*
- *"You're by no means perfect, you know!"*

What to Do
- If you hear the same criticism about yourself several times, from different people, take a careful look at yourself; perhaps the criticism has at least a grain of truth in it.
- Counter every negative thing the person says with a positive comment.

Don't . . .
- . . . join in on or agree with the criticism about yourself or others.
- . . . let unfair criticisms affect your self-esteem.
- . . . criticize the criticizer in return.

The Person with a "Poor Me" Attitude

It is certainly normal for someone to be in a negative, 'poor me' state of mind when he or she is having a bad day or going through a crisis. This section is for people who constantly see themselves as helpless victims of the everyday mishaps of life—like getting a paper cut or getting cut off in traffic or being rained on. Even when something supposedly good happens, to this person, it is only a prelude to the next disaster. Hopefully your comments and actions will help this person to see that not everything is negative!

What to Say
- *"Remember that God loves you and is on your side, no matter what!"*
- *"I try to find the positive in any situation, and here's what I see that is positive about what's happening in your life right now . . ."*

- *"You woke up this morning, and I see you're able to walk and talk and breathe without assistance . . . "*
- If the self-pity gets ridiculous, you might say, *"Well, they can't take away your birthday!"* or, *"They probably won't eat you, and that's a good thing!"*
- Sometimes gentle sarcasm helps get the point across; *"You're right, it is totally hopeless. Nothing will ever be positive ever again in the whole world."*
- *"For you, it's been a totally rotten, no good, terribly bad, day/week/month."*
- Point out reality; *"You've got a loving family, nice home, job you enjoy . . . "*

What Not to Say
- Anything cruel, like, *"You're such a loser, aren't you."*

What to Do
- Give your replies and comments with patience and respect; ask God to help you do so.
- Listen for a few minutes; sometimes just talking will help the person get the negativity out of his system and begin to feel better.
- Encourage someone who seems discouraged or down to trust God and reach out to Him.
- Remind the person of someone else who has been through difficult circumstances, not to diminish what he is going through, but to point out the reality that there are people who are in more difficult situations.
- Encourage the person to volunteer at a hospital, nursing home, or rehabilitation hospital; helping others makes us feel better about ourselves and may help someone to see the good in his or her life.
- Encourage him to make a list of five things, every day, that he is thankful for.

Don't . . .
- . . . start a 'my life is worse than your life' contest, trying to point out how your life is worse than his.

The Person Who Curses in Public

Before you confront someone in public, consider the circumstances. If someone is uninhibited enough to raise his voice and use inappropriate language in public, he probably would not hesitate to make a scene if you bring up his choice of words, especially if he is inebriated or angry. If you choose to approach the person about his behavior, do so calmly.

If the person is a family member or someone you see frequently, speak with him in private, asking him to curb his language around you and your family.

What to Say
- *"I find that word offensive; please don't use it when I'm around."*
- *"We're trying to teach our children not to use those words. Could you please help by not using them when the kids are around?"*
- *"That is my Savior you are cursing."*
- *"Would you please tone down the words? My kids repeat everything to my mother-in-law and I don't want her to think I said that!"*
- If your children are with you, say something to them like, *"That man's mom didn't teach him what words he shouldn't say. He says them, but if you say them you will be punished!"*

What Not to Say
- *"Don't you have any sense whatsoever?"*

What to Do
- Make your remark calmly, with a neutral expression and tone of voice. If you make a joke of it, the person (and your kids) won't take your request seriously; if you act angry, the situation could escalate.

- Consider reminding the person of God's commandment that we not take his name in vain.

Don't . . .
- . . . risk a confrontation with someone who looks very angry or could be inebriated.

Someone Who is Always Experiencing a Crisis

Some individuals seem to thrive on crisis, and therefore make every problem—whether it's the fact that she can't find her keys, doesn't know what to cook for supper, or is afraid she accidentally might have offended someone—into a minor (or major!) crisis. There are several underlying reasons a person might act this way.

The person may be insecure, and need approval for even the smallest decision she makes; by making it into a crisis, she will get input from others on what the right solution is.

A person might operate in crisis mode so he can avoid the real problems and issues in his life; it is easier for him to focus on the 'crisis' of his favorite bagel shop closing, than to think about the fact that his child has been arrested twice in the last month for drug possession.

Some people simply enjoy the attention they get when they are in the midst of a crisis; therefore, they are constantly experiencing some type of crisis.

Your response will probably be similar no matter what you feel the underlying motives (conscious or unconscious) for the 'crisis' are.

What to Say
To the person who is avoiding a true crisis (be cautious speculating if you don't know the person, or the details of his situation, well);
- *"Are you really so upset that the price of gas went up again, or are you worried about your mom's illness?"*

- *"So many relatively minor things seem to bother you. Have you thought about talking to someone professional to see if there's something more behind all of your concerns?"*

To the person who is insecure;
- *"What do you think we should do?"* Praise good solutions he proposes and perhaps he will gain confidence in making his own decisions.

If you are not sure of the motives behind the person who is always having a crisis;
- *"What do you think you should do?"*
- *"I have 10 minutes before I have to get back to work, but I'll listen until then!"*
- *"Do you want my suggestions, or do you just need to talk about it?"* (Listen, and then give suggestions if asked.)
- If the person disregards your suggestions and does not seem to want to solve the problem, say, *"I've given you my suggestions; I don't have any more! I guess you'll just have to do what you feel is best."*

What Not to Say
- *"You are such a complainer—can't you figure out anything on your own?"*
- *"The solution to that is simple—can't you see it?"*
- *"Here's what you've got to do . . ."*

What to Do
- Realize that you don't always have to offer a solution; many times the person will come up with a solution (if he or she wants to) after just talking through his options.
- If asked, give your suggestions; even if the solution appears clear to you, it might not be to the person in the midst of the crisis.
- Distance yourself from the situation if you are spending more time and energy trying to find solutions, than the person in the midst of the crisis is.

- A person may not realize he or she is creating crisis after crisis to avoid real problems, and probably will deny it (and possibly get angry) if you suggest that he is. Consider suggesting the person see a professional who can help.

Don't . . .
- . . . offer suggestions if the person just wants to talk about the problem.
- . . . get sucked into expending large amounts of time or energy on small problems.
- . . . worry more about the situation than the person with the crisis does.
- . . . feel responsible for solving the person's problems.

When Someone Won't Take Responsibility for His or Her Problems

Some people refuse to take responsibility for the problems that result from their bad choices, poor decisions, and irresponsible actions. They continually blame others, or circumstances supposedly beyond their control, for the negative things that are happening in their lives.

These individuals create great consternation among friends and family and those around them, yet will not take steps to improve the situation; sometimes they even seem to do things that make the situation worse. You might realize this after the person has come to you several times in the midst of a crisis, and despite efforts to help and encouragement from yourself and others to improve the situation, the person refuses to take any steps which would resolve the problem or at least improve the situation.

If you are putting more time, thought, worry, and effort into trying to solve someone else's problems, than he is, or if his predicaments are taking you away from your family, or you notice negative changes in your personality or health from being too closely involved, it's time to step back from the situation and decide what actions you can take to truly help.

First of all, ask God to help you see the situation clearly and enable you to discern His will in the situation. If the person does not truly want to take the (sometimes difficult) steps to make the situation better, nothing you do will help. In fact, if you continue to try to help and support him, you might be enabling him to continue his damaging behavior.

It is difficult to step back from a friendship, but sometimes necessary for the well-being of your friend, and for your own well-being. Above all, act and speak with compassion in this difficult situation. Here are some suggestions for what to say and do.

What to Say
- *"I've tried to help you come up with solutions to your problems, but you don't seem willing to consider any of them . . ."*
- *"I hate to see you hurting yourself by doing the same things over and over!"*
- *"Look at the choices you've made in the past, and their consequences. You're faced with a similar choice now—what are you going to do to assure a better outcome this time?"*
- *"You've made some bad choices in the past, but you can turn it around!"*
- *"Your situation is not going to improve unless you make some changes."*
- *"What do you think God would want you to do in this situation?"*
- *"Have you prayed about this decision?"*
- *"I am not qualified to give you the help you need. I'm going to continue to urge you to get professional help—I would not be a friend if I did not urge you to do what you need to do."*
- *"I just can't talk to you about that situation anymore unless you're willing to do something to try to fix it."*

What Not to Say
- *"Your situation is hopeless."*
- *"Don't bother to come to me anymore about this."*
- *"You'll never change."*

What to Do
- Pray for the right words to say to your friend, and for the wisdom to know when and how to distance yourself, if necessary.
- Remember that God loves your friend; let His love show through in what you do and say.
- Try to help your friend see how her choices/actions/decisions have resulted in her current circumstances.
- Offer to make an appointment for the person to see a counselor or clergy person; offer to take the person to, or go with her to the appointment.
- If you distance yourself from the person, consider maintaining a superficial friendship; perhaps in the future the friendship can be strong again.

Don't . . .
- . . . stay in, or be drawn back into the friendship through guilt.
- . . . completely cut off all ties, if that is possible.

Getting Along with Someone Whose Company You do Not Enjoy

There will always be people who rub you the wrong way, but can't be avoided—co-workers, people at church, even family members. The person might have mannerisms or eccentricities that are irritating (to you), or be difficult to make conversation with. Maybe the person is self-centered, obnoxious, or has a lifestyle that is very different that yours, perhaps demonstrating his or her differing values. Perhaps you have little or nothing in common. Maybe there isn't a concrete reason you don't get along with the person, you just do not enjoy his or her company. How do you handle those inevitable times you have to interact?

Here are suggestions for interacting with someone whose company you don't enjoy.

What to Say
- *"Nice weather!"*
- *"How about that game last week?"*
- *"What are you doing this weekend?"*
- *"Did you see the TV show last night?" " Did you see the movie everyone is talking about? What did you think about it?" "Have you read the new bestseller?"*
- About the event you're at; *"The hostess did a great job of arranging this event." "The food is yummy, isn't it?" "How do you know the boss?"*

What Not to Say
- *"Are you able to get along with* anyone*?"*
- *"You're really hard to talk to!"*
- *"I'd rather be anywhere but here talking to you!"*

What to Do
- Pray for God's love to flow through you and for Him to give you grace and a kind heart to handle the situation.
- Remind yourself that even people who annoy you are loved and valued by God. He loves all of us, in spite of our personalities.
- Consider the possible reasons behind the person's behavior—perhaps she had extremely critical parents, has very low self-confidence, or had a troubled childhood or difficult relationships throughout life. Circumstances do not excuse unacceptable behavior, but will help you see the person's traits with compassion.
- Remember God's commandment to love your neighbor as yourself. Perhaps you have been put into each other's lives for a reason.
- Be open-minded—try to find a positive quality in the person.
- If you know you'll have to interact with the person, at a meal, meeting, or conference, for example, think of several things to talk about. If it's someone you see at your child's school, make a comment about the artwork on the walls or the upcoming field trip. If it's someone at church, mention the music that was played during the service. If it's a co-worker, say something about

work. The weather is always a safe subject, whether it's hot, cold, rainy, dry, windy, humid, snowy. Or talk about the local sports team, perhaps bringing up their last game or the upcoming season. Planning ahead will help you get through uncomfortable encounters.
- Make an honest effort to get to know the person; you might find you really do enjoy his or her company.

Don't . . .
- . . . criticize the person to others, after talking to him.
- . . . pretend to approve of bad behavior like sexist jokes or cursing, in an attempt to get along.

Chapter Four

Family

Most families have some sort of dysfunction; some families put the "fun" into dysfunction, while others put the "funk" into dysfunctional! Some people (and the situations that arise because of their dysfunction) are amusing, some are annoying, and some are harmful to other family members.

Long histories with each other, complicated relationships, and past hurts and misunderstandings all come into play when dealing with difficult family members. It can be difficult to know how to react to, or act on, family situations.

If a family member—your family member, your spouse's, or a friend's—acts inappropriately, consider the reasons that might be behind that behavior. Some behaviors—butting into every conversation, for example—might be attributed to loneliness. If you suspect a relative is lonely, show compassion and give him some attention, even if his behaviors make it hard.

Other behaviors, like talking too loudly, repeating the same statement over and over, or making bizarre, off-the-subject comments, could be the result of a medical process like hearing loss or the first stages of dementia. Dozing off during a conversation, walking unsteadily, frequently asking to go to the bathroom, or incontinency, or similar behaviors, could be side effects of medications the person is taking. Consider these possibilities before attributing inappropriate behaviors to the person's personality.

If you think a medical reason might be behind the behavior, encourage the person to see a doctor, or suggest a doctor visit to family members who are in charge of taking the person to the doctor.

If you've ruled out other causes, and the inappropriate behavior is from years of 'practice,' you'll have to approach it in a different way.

Your Own Family

Family problems may be centered on one troublesome family member, one branch of the family tree (a sibling and his or her spouse and children, for example), or behavior patterns of the entire family.

Most likely, troublesome behaviors (regardless of the number of family members who exhibit them), have been ingrained through years of 'practice' (being allowed to act that way without consequences). Sometimes long-ago events or misunderstandings cause tension and are part of the cause of bad behaviors. If this is the case, it will probably be very difficult to actually change the dysfunctional patterns. You might have to make a decision between gritting your teeth and putting up with the behaviors, or pulling away from the people taking part in these destructive behaviors.

Before you approach a family member about his or her actions and behaviors, ask yourself if the potential upheaval that confronting the issue is worth it. This depends on many factors. Does this member of the family live far away or close to you? Do you see him often or rarely? Do positive character traits outweigh the negative? Is the person's behavior merely annoying, or truly destructive to one or more family members? Does the family allow the behaviors to continue, perpetuating the hurt? Even family members should not be permitted to be involved in your life to the extent or in a manner of causing damage to another's physical and/or emotional health.

If you see the problem-causing person frequently, and the behavior occurs often, or is very hurtful to other family members, you may feel you have to take action to protect your family. Do not hesitate to stand up for yourself, your family or other extended family members, or your beliefs. Future negative memories are not worth 'keeping the peace.'

On the other hand, if the behavior is more irritating than hurtful, or if you rarely see the person, or if his or her positive characteristics that outweigh the negative, it may be better to tolerate it during the infrequent times you are together. You can do this with 'superficial friendliness'—greet the person politely, make a few minutes of small talk, as required, and then manage to keep your distance from the person.

General Guidelines for Dealing with Dysfunctional Family Members

What to Say

Consider talking with a family member about unacceptable behaviors, or resolving past misunderstandings, before you get together for an event.

- *"Uncle Jim, I know you love to tell jokes, but some are really off-color, and our kids are getting old enough to understand and repeat them. Could you please keep it G-rated at our Thanksgiving dinner next week? We would really appreciate it."*
- *"My children and the other little ones at family dinners get very upset when you tease them about their hair color or being overweight. I know you don't mean to hurt their feelings, but you do with those comments. This year at the reunion, could you please not do that? The kids would love for you to ask them how their softball team is doing, or about our vacation. Thank you for understanding!"*
- *"What happened between us was a long time ago. Can we start with a clean slate at the family get-together next month?"*
- *"I want to apologize for my part in our misunderstanding last year. I would like to try to repair our friendship and hope we can start at the family dinner next week."*

If old issues or disagreements come up during an event, try these replies:

- *"Let's just not talk about that, but celebrate the wedding. That's what we're here for."*
- *"Let's enjoy being together and not talk about old hurts now."*
- *"I'm sorry you're still angry about what happened, but I cannot change it. I just want to get along for the sake of our parents and kids."*

What Not to Say
- *"You're such a jerk!"*
- *"You've been this way since we were kids!"*
- *"You always act this way."*
- *"Mom and dad always let you get away with everything. That's why you are like this."*
- *"It's all your fault that our family is like this."*
- *"I still can't believe you did that to me 20 years ago . . . "*

What to Do
- Pray for guidance about what to say and do, and for patience, kindness, and understanding in dealing with the issue.
- Tell the truth with love and kindness.
- Plan ahead for what you'll do and say if certain situations occur; you might try to diffuse an argument, separate people who are arguing, step away from someone who is harassing you, etc.
- Be proactive; enlist other family members to either help resolve disputes or separate trouble-makers if disputes start at a get-together.

Don't . . .
- . . . fall into old patterns with family members.
- . . . have unrealistic expectations of family members changing or getting along, even if you've talked with the people involved and the conflicts seem to be resolved.
- . . . be afraid to make a scene if necessary, if someone is being hurt physically or emotionally.

Here are suggestions for dealing with family members in specific situations that may come up.

If You Don't Want to Stay at a Family Member's Home

To reduce tension at family get-togethers, consider spending evenings and nights at a hotel.

What to Say
- "We will stay at a hotel because we get up a lot during the night and don't want to disturb you."
- "We couldn't possibly stay in your home and disrupt your routine!"
- "It's way too much of an imposition to stay with you in your home."
- "Your house will be crowded with so many people there; we will stay at a hotel."
- "Things get tense if we're together too much; we'll stay overnight in a hotel. It will be better for everyone if we have a little time apart."
- "I've developed an allergy to dogs/cats/hamsters/flowers and the doctor said I can't be around them for more than a few hours at a time."
- "We want everyone to have a great time on this vacation; to make sure we're rested up for everything we'll stay in a hotel."

What Not to Say
- "We just can't stand to spend that many hours in a row near you." (Be kind!)
- "Um, we were, ah, thinking about, just maybe, considering possibly staying in a hotel." (State your decision clearly so there are no doubts about your plans.)

What to Do
- Present staying in a hotel as being a favor to the people you are visiting.
- Tell the person of your plans to stay in a hotel in advance so she doesn't spend time preparing a room for you.
- If the person would be very hurt by your not staying with them, consider staying at their home but for a shorter visit.

Don't . . .
- . . . be 'guilted' into staying at someone's home if it's not the best option for your family.

If You Don't Want Family Members to Stay at Your Home

What to Say
- *"With limited space at our home, it's hard to make sure everyone is comfortable."*
- *"We want your vacation to be wonderful and think you'd be more comfortable sleeping at a hotel."*
- *"Our plumbing just can't handle too many people . . ."*
- *"We get up a lot during the night; I think you'd be able to rest better at a hotel."*

What Not to Say
- *"We just can't stand to be around you that many hours without a break! You have to stay at a hotel!"*

What to Do
- Consider paying all or part of the expense of the hotel.
- Negotiate them staying a shorter time if they refuse to stay in a hotel.

Don't . . .
- . . . be 'guilted' into letting someone stay at your home if it's not best for your family.

Limiting Contact or Cutting Ties with a Family Member

The decision to limit contact or cut all ties with a family member or members is a difficult one and should not be made in haste or without a lot of thought and prayer. Situations in which you may choose to cut off contact temporarily or permanently may include abuse (towards yourself or someone else), violence, drug or alcohol abuse, damaging manipulative behavior, living an immoral lifestyle, and/or criminal behavior.

If you or other family members are in danger, or discover something extremely troubling about the person (that he has sexually abused someone, for example), you'll probably leave that person's presence immediately. Whether you see the person again depends on the specifics of the situation and if the person is remorseful and makes amends.

If your seeing the person again depends on specific things he or she does or does not do, make that clear to the person face to face, over the phone, or by mail or e-mail, depending on the specifics of situation. Your priority is keeping yourself and your family safe. Do not put yourself in danger.

What to Say
- *"I will not be around you if you are using illegal drugs."*
- *"When you were so angry last week, I was afraid you were going to physically hurt someone. You will not be invited to our home again until and unless you get your temper under control. I think you need professional help and hope you get it. Call me when you are able to be with us without getting so angry."*
- *"Hitting your spouse is wrong, and you are not welcome in our home until you get professional help. You and your wife are in our prayers."*
- *"Your actions with that child are absolutely unacceptable. It is not safe for you to be around children, and we will not be around you unless and until you accept you have a problem and are able to control it."*

- *"Every time we're together dad gets angry about something, overreacts, calls names, and ruins the occasion. I'm not going to let him set such a negative example for our children; we want them to remember holidays as fun events, not stressful ones. We will not be spending any holidays with him until and unless he changes his behavior."*
- When talking with the person exhibiting the behaviors, set firm limits; *"In the past, your behavior with family members has been inappropriate and rude. It doesn't matter why you continue to act that way even after we've talked about it and you've promised to not act that way. I want to have a relationship with you, but cannot and will not do that unless and until you treat us with respect. That means no yelling, name calling, or critical remarks. If you continue to treat us inappropriately, we will not be able to be in the same place at the same time. You will not intimidate or hurt me or my family any more."*

What Not to Say
- *"Your behavior is horrible and we can't stand to be around you."* (Instead of saying this, point out specific behaviors that are unacceptable to you.)

What to Do
- Pray for God's guidance as to what to do to protect yourself and your family.
- Consider asking another family member or friend to be present while you talk to the person about his or her negative behaviors.
- Be calm and objective when you talk with the person about his behavior.
- Consider attending at least part of a family event, even if you suspect you'll have to leave early due to the behavior of another person. If the situation takes a turn for the worse, it's OK to leave. Sometimes it takes a dramatic event—like part of the family leaving right in the middle of dinner—for the person causing the problem, and the rest of the family, to realize the damage that person is causing. The statement you make by leaving might give

the rest of the family the courage to take a stand of their own, or pressure the trouble-maker to act in an acceptable manner.

Don't ...
- ... continue relationships that are harmful or dangerous to yourself or your family.

Explaining Your Actions to Other Family Members

It's probably not necessary to tell distant, rarely-seen relatives, every detail of why you've decided to limit contact with a family member or not attend an event. However, if the person you are avoiding could be a danger to others, you have an obligation to share relevant details so others can protect themselves and their families. If family get-togethers have been contentious for years, others will probably understand (even if they do not like the fact that you are pulling away), without your outlining the details, your decision not to attend an event or get together.

If the conflict was not common knowledge, you have to decide how many and which of the details to share. Before you do so, consider your motives—is it really necessary to share every detail, or are you sharing unnecessary details for revenge or to 'prove' you were 'right' about something?

The following examples will give you ideas for dealing with this situation.

What to Say
- To an elderly aunt whom you rarely see, when she asks why you didn't attend the reunion the previous summer; *"It just didn't work out for us last year. But we hope to see you very soon!"*
- A cousin with whom you're close; *"My sister and I have a difficult relationship, and it's best if we're not together at family gatherings. Her behaviors towards my family hurt them deeply, and I'm not going to ask them to put themselves through that. We're sorry to miss the get-together but have to this year."*
- To your brother, whose wife disrupts holiday gatherings; *"I'm sorry to have to say this, but your wife's behavior at family events is just too disruptive. She makes fun of our children and made*

mom cry with her cruel remarks last year. If she will not promise to not yell or make critical comments this year, I'm afraid we can't invite her."
- To your mother; *"It's just too hard to be around my brother when he constantly reminds me of mistakes I made years ago. I've asked him over and over not to bring them up, but he continues to. I'm not going to come to the wedding this summer because I'm not going to put myself through that again."*
- *"The last three holiday dinners have ended in tears. Our family is going to spend it alone this year; we're not inviting anyone."*

What Not to Say
- *"He is a jerk and no one should be around him."*
- *"If you care about me you won't go to the reunion either."*
- *"We're not coming and you should know why."*
- *"Whatever she says is a lie. You better not listen, if you want to be friends with me."*

What to Do
- Prayerfully consider the actions that are best for you and your family.
- Tell others of your decision objectively and calmly.
- Tell other family members of potentially harmful behaviors like violence, sexual abuse, or criminal activity.
- Consider giving more details to someone who can and will try to do something about the disruptive family member.
- Remember that family dynamics are complicated and can be unpredictable; people who could do something about the troubling family member, for a variety of reasons, might not be willing to do so.
- Be prepared for any reaction from the person you bring into the situation—he could be willing to help, or become very defensive and angry at you.

Don't . . .
- . . . ask people to take sides in the conflict.
- . . . be vengeful in what you say; tell only the truth.

- ... second-guess your decision if family members tell you that you are 'over-reacting' or wrong to pull back from other family members. Your priority is to protect yourself and your family.

The Embarrassing Family Member

In almost every family there is someone who talks too loudly in public, can be counted on to say just the *wrong* (usually embarrassing) thing at the wrong time, insults your friends, yells at you in front of other people, does anything to be the center of attention, or otherwise makes a spectacle of him or herself.

Remember that these actions are usually more noticeable to you than to people around you, who might not even notice the inappropriate behavior. If no one else seems to have noticed, just ignore what the person said or did. If, however, it is clear that the person made a scene, here are some things you can say and do.

What to Say
- Roll your eyes and say, *"He must have forgotten to take his medications this morning."*
- With a little smile, say, *"There's one in every family!"*
- *"She takes the 'fun' right out of dysfunctional."*
- *"It's so embarrassing when she does that! She just doesn't realize what she's doing is not appropriate."*

If your family member has embarrassed someone or hurt their feelings, say,
- *"I'm so sorry for what she just said to you! She just doesn't realize how inappropriate comments like that are."*
- *"I cannot control what he says, but I certainly don't share his views and I'm so sorry he said that to you."*

What Not to Say
- *"He is such a jerk!"* (This might be true, but saying it just makes the situation worse.)

What to Do
- With a smile, shake your head and roll your eyes.
- If the family member is in the middle of creating a scene, try to diffuse the situation by changing the subject or suggesting, *"Let's go get something to eat,"* or finding a way to leave the scene.

Don't . . .
- . . . cry, yell, or get overly emotional; this just draws more attention to the situation and makes people uncomfortable.
- . . . dwell on what happened; that also draws more attention to the situation and makes others uncomfortable.

If Someone Makes Sexual Comments or Advances

Sexual comments or inappropriate advances might be part of a person's behavior, but if they make you uncomfortable, speak up!

What to Say
- *"That's not an appropriate thing to say to me."*
- *"Your comments about my body make me uncomfortable—please don't make them anymore."*
- *"Do not touch me like that."*
- *"What would your wife think of you saying that?"*

What Not to Say
- *"Um, please, do you think, uh, you could maybe not say things like that?"*
- *"You're a really nasty person."*

What to Do
- Tell your spouse about the inappropriate actions or comments, and carefully consider telling other family members.
- Remember that offensive behaviors could be due to medications or a medical condition like dementia.
- Set clear limits with a person who is being inappropriate; *"Do not touch me like that or make lewd comments to me."*

Don't . . .
- . . . allow inappropriate touching or comments, even if you have to make a 'scene.'
- . . . be alone with the person.

Your Spouse's Family

Ideally, your spouse should handle problems if his or her parents or other family members are acting inappropriately. However, this is not always the case. If behavior patterns are long-standing, your spouse may not realize they are not appropriate, or, due to family dynamics, your spouse might not be willing to risk the consequences of confronting a problem. It might be up to you to take action. When you show your spouse that you are determined to protect your family, he or she will probably be relieved, and your actions might empower him to take a stand with his parents or other family members.

Before you say or do anything, pray about it, and talk with your spouse about possible solutions. If the two of you cannot agree on a plan of action, you have several options. If the actions of the troublemaker aren't hurting your children or spouse physically, emotionally, or spiritually, grit your teeth and bear family get-togethers for the sake of your marriage. If the behaviors *are* causing damage, you are obligated to protect your children from the situation. Consider talking with your pastor, priest, or a counselor about the situation and your best plan of action.

A Friend's Family

When a Friend is Having Family Difficulties
The category of "family difficulties" includes any sort of conflict with extended family members or in-laws. The problem could me major—a long-standing disagreement—or minor—a misunderstanding about a party invitation, for example. Whether the problem is small or large, important or trivial, it's causing stress for your

friend, and it's helpful to her to have someone outside the family to listen when she wants to talk.

What to Say
- *"I will pray for you!" "What would you like me to pray for?"*
- *"Would you like to tell me what happened?"*
- *"How are things going this week?"*
- *"I can tell you're trying really hard to resolve this."*
- If she suggests a solution to resolve the problem, and it sounds like a good one to you, *"That sounds like a great solution!"*
- If she suggests a solution that doesn't sound like it would be productive, *"Are you sure that's something that you want to do? I don't want it to backfire on you, or make things worse."*
- If she is upset about something that was said about her, that you have not seen to be true, *"I know you are a great mother, even if your mom said you're not."*
- Offer your objective opinion, gently, *"I looked at your sister offering to help as caring for you, not as putting you down." "It is sad that they play favorites with their grandchildren, buy you've mentioned them doing that before, so it is their pattern of behavior."*

What Not to Say
- *"You should not feel that way!"*
- *"Here's just what you need to do . . . "*
- *"Don't let them do that to you!"* (She has no control over how anyone else acts.)
- *"You should have seen that coming before you married him."*

What to Do
- Be very careful about going with your friend to confront family members about a problem; there are probably family dynamics you are not aware of and the reaction of family members is not predictable. In most cases it's better to let a professional be a mediator.
- Be cautious when offering advice; you don't know all the aspects of both sides of the conflict or the family dynamics involved. If

you do have suggestions, offer them gently, *"What do you think would happen if you . . . " "Have you thought of trying . . . "*
- If the problem is long-lasting or affecting your friend negatively over a long period of time, suggest that she talk with a pastor, priest, or counselor.
- Realize that sometimes ongoing conflict is just part of how a family functions; if one conflict is resolved, another will be created.

Don't . . .
- . . . criticize the other family members; it's OK to listen to your friend talk about them, but don't add to add your criticisms to hers.
- . . . go behind your friend's back and try to "fix" the problem with other family members. It could backfire and damage your relationship with your friend.
- . . . gossip about their family problems to other people.
- . . . shrink away from listening to your friend talk about family conflicts or painful memories of abuse or cruelty from family members. It's hard to listen to, but it's important for your friend to talk about it and to know you accept her despite what has happened.
- . . . become too involved; if you worry and think about it more than she does, or she is reluctant to consider any type of help, you might need to step back. However, if the person you are avoiding could be a danger to others, you have an obligation to share relevant details so others can protect themselves and their families. Sometimes ongoing conflict is just a part of how a family functions.

When a Friend Cuts Ties, or Limits Contact, with a Family Member

If a family feud cause a friend to take a drastic action, like move away from her extended family, cut off ties, or not allow the grandparents see their grandchildren, do not judge her actions. You might not consider taking such actions, but your friend obviously felt it was very necessary. Accept her feelings (anger, sadness, relief) about what was probably a difficult decision for her.

What to Say
- *"I'm sorry you are having such a difficult time with your family!"*
- *"I know your uncle, and his behavior does not change our friendship or what I think about you."*
- *"I respect you for taking the measures you have to protect your family."*
- *"Do you want to tell me what led you to make that decision?"* (The person might feel uncomfortable talking with you about the situation unless you show her you're willing to listen.)
- If a relative is making a public scene and your friend is handling the situation, say to anyone watching, *"Let's give them some privacy. The family has it handled."*

What Not to Say
- *"You shouldn't do that!"*
- *"You should have done _____ instead."*
- *"You should have tried harder."*
- *"Can you believe this? What a family!"*
- *"Your family is really messed up!"*
- *"You should do something about your family."*

What to Do
- Pray for your friend and her family.
- Reassure your friend that the actions of her family members do not affect your friendship or how you feel about her.
- Reassure you friend that you respect the actions she takes in regards to her extended family.
- Allow your friend to cry, complain , yell about the situation; accept her feelings and emotions.
- Invite your friend and her family to your own holiday celebrations if you know they won't be spending holidays with their own extended family members.

Don't . . .
- . . . judge your friend's actions.
- . . . gossip to other people about your friend's family.
- . . . chastise or argue with your friend's family members

When a Friend's Elderly Relative Needs More Care
A friend faces many issues when a relative needs more care. Many family dynamics are involved, including your friend's relationship with the relative who needs more care, as well as her relationship with siblings or other relatives who might feel they have a say in the decision.

What to Say
- *"You're in my prayers as you're dealing with this."*
- *"This must be a difficult decision for you."*
- *"I know you'll do what is right for your dad."*
- *"This must be a stressful time for you."* (This opens the door for her to talk—or not—about any aspect of what is going on.)
- *"You're doing a great job in a difficult situation."*
- *"How are your brothers and sisters dealing with all of this?"*
- *"You are doing the right thing; from what you have told me, it is not safe for her to live alone."*
- *"I can recommend _____"* (facility) (if you have first-hand knowledge of the facility).
- *"That facility has a very good reputation; she will be safe and well-cared for there."*

What Not to Say
- *"I just saw your aunt and she was fine—why can't you check in on her every day and keep her at home?"* (You don't have first-hand knowledge of the situation and don't know all of the reasons behind the decision.)
- *"Can't he just move in with you or one of your sisters?"*
- *"You shouldn't do that to her."*

What to Do
- Pray for your friend to be led to make the right decision; pray for her peace of mind.
- Let your friend talk, and accept her feelings, which may include anger, confusion, guilt, relief.
- E-mail your friend with words of encouragement.
- Give your friend information about local services like Meals on Wheels, Hospice, etc.
- Share any personal experiences with a facility in which your friend is considering placing her relative, especially if your experiences were positive. If you have first-hand, objective knowledge that there are facility-wide problems, making it unsafe, tell you friend that also.

Don't ...
- ... share negative stereotypes about long-term-care or assisted-living facilities.
- ... criticize your friend's decisions.

When Someone's Elderly Relative is in a Long-Term Care Unit
- *"Have you seen your mom lately?"* (Asking the question in this way allows the person to go into as little or as much detail as she wants to.)
- If the relative is in declining health or doesn't recognize family members, say, *"This must be difficult for you."*
- If the person didn't recognize your friend, or said something inappropriate or mean, *"Remember, his mind is not working right."*
- *"I've been thinking of you lately." "I know you're dealing with a lot right now."* (Sometimes answering a question about how a relative is doing can seem almost overwhelming; a statement shows your concern and your friend doesn't have to try to condense a lot of information into a brief answer.)
- *"You did the right thing in making sure she is safe."*
- *"Is she up to visitors? Can I visit? Can I take her anything?"*

What Not to Say
- *"You should have flowers in her room/bring your dad home for the holidays/ take him cookies/visit more often/open the curtains."* (When a person has dementia things he or she normally enjoys may agitate him or her. Also remember that there are family dynamics that may go back many years, details that you are not even aware of, influencing your friend and his loved one.)
- *"That's not a good place for him."*

What to Do
- Do not ask about your friend's loved one unless you are willing to listen to her talk; if you don't truly care, she will be able to sense that.
- Know that sometimes your friend might not want to talk about her loved one; it might be too painful or she might just be emotionally tired of the situation and not want to discuss it.
- Allow your friend to express her feelings and emotions—anger, tears, relief, confusion, etc. Accept her feelings; all are normal.
- If the relative's condition changes (he is diagnosed with Alzheimer's Disease, or breaks a hip, for example), and you have first-hand knowledge, suggest a facility which specializes in that disease or offers a higher level of care.

Don't . . .
- . . . tell anyone how they 'should' handle a situation, how often they should visit, etc.
- . . . judge the amount of time the person spends visiting his or her loved one.

Chapter 5

Death

There are few times in life when it's more important to put our own feelings aside and look at the needs of another, as when someone has experienced the death of a loved one. Your actions and words can help or hinder the grief process.

Many times our automatic responses, the things that are easy to say and do, are an attempt to deal with our own discomfort; the words and deeds that will truly help and comfort someone who is grieving can be much more difficult to say and do. Some of the suggestions below might seem contrary to what seems 'right', so reasons for the responses are included.

When Someone's Loved One has Died

In the First Hours and Days After a Loved one Has Died

A person who has lost a loved one through death will probably experience a wide range of emotions. Depending on the circumstances, these emotions can include grief, anger (even anger at the person who has died), relief (if the person who died had been suffering or his relationship with others was not good), ambivalence, and fear. The grieving person might laugh, cry, scream, be completely silent, or want to talk. Let her experience and express whatever emotions she is feeling; that is normal and part of the healing process. It's hard to see a friend in such distress, but put aside your own discomfort (it's not about you!) and be there for your friend.

What to Say
- *"I'm so very sorry!"*
- *"Is there anyone you would like me to call to tell them the news, or ask them to come and be with you?"*
- *"I cannot take away your pain, but I can and will be here for you."*
- *"No matter what happens, I know you can handle it."*
- *"She is in heaven now."*
- *""He's free of all pain, now."*
- *"She is with God now."*
- *"God is taking care of you and your family; He loves you all very much."*
- *"Would you like to talk about what happened?"* (This is a good open-ended question; the person can tell you as much or as little as she wants about the circumstances surrounding the death. Allow her to talk about it as much as she wants, even if it makes you uncomfortable; talking about it helps the bereaved person to process the event and is an important part of the healing process.)
- *"Would you like to see him?"* (meaning the person who has died). If the answer is *"yes,"* ask, *"Would you like me to go with you, or do you want privacy?"*
- A person who has lost a spouse will probably be overwhelmed by his or her added responsibilities related to children, a business, etc. Reassure him; *"Yes, you can take care of the children yourself; it will be hard, but there are many people who love you and will help. You can do it!"*
- If you are at the hospital and feel qualified, act as a go-between with the doctors and nurses and grieving person. Ask, *"Is there anything you want to ask the doctors or nurses, or talk with them about?"*

If the person expresses guilt or remorse over the circumstances that led to the death, or things said or not said, things done or not done, say one of the following things:
- *"You could not have prevented this!"*
- *"You could not have known this would happen!"*
- *"He would not want you to feel guilty about what happened."*
- *"She knows how much you loved her; you showed it over the years you were together."*

If you are a close friend or relative, you might have to take the role of guiding the person through the process of signing papers, making a decision about organ donation, calling the funeral home, and so on. Gently guide by saying,
- *"We need to make a decision about donating her organs. Did she ever share her feelings about organ donation? Do you have any questions about it?"*
- *"It's time to call the funeral home. Which one do you want to use? Would you like me to make the call?"*

If you are not sure of the deceased person's beliefs, or the survivor expresses sadness because he is uncertain if the person had a relationship with God, say;
- *"Regardless of his beliefs, he will live on forever here,"* (motion toward your head), *"and here."* (put your hands on your heart).
- It is OK to say nothing; just be there.

What Not to Say

Often our discomfort with death prompts us to say *something, anything,* rather than saying nothing. Unfortunately, things you say to cover up your own painful emotions, or fill a silence, can be inappropriate and even hurtful. Don't say these things; it is better to be silent.
- *"Don't cry!"* People say this because they are uncomfortable with displays of extreme emotion. A grieving person needs to cry! Don't let your discomfort prompt you to stifle this need.
- *"Don't say that!"* The grieving person needs to express his or her emotions. If he says something that is obviously untrue, like,

"She was mad at me and that's why she died!" correct it with facts; *"Your emotions did not cause the accident."*
- *"I know just exactly how you feel."* Even if you've been in a similar situation (your grandfather died during surgery for cancer, just like your friend's grandfather), your feelings will not be exactly the same as the person who is currently grieving.
- *"You shouldn't feel that way!"* There is no 'wrong' way to feel when you are grieving!
- *"He's better off now so don't be sad."* Even if the grieving person realizes this is the truth, saying it implies he is selfish for feeling sad about the death. However, if the grieving person expresses this sentiment, it's OK to agree.
- *"Was he a Christian?"* You appear to be judging the person if he was not.
- *"Everything will turn out to be perfectly fine; don't you worry a bit!"* Obviously things will not be 'perfectly fine'!

What to Do
- Sit with the person while he cries, talks, or just sits silently. Many times your heartfelt, comforting, silent presence is the best comfort.
- Offer to call a clergy person.
- If you are a close friend or relative, consider asking a doctor or nurse for details of the death so you can relate them to the grieving person at a later time (the person who is grieving may not remember what he or she had been told immediately after the death). Privacy laws prohibit the medical staff from sharing any of these details unless they have permission from the immediate family of the person who has died, so ask the nurse or doctor in the presence of someone from the immediate family.
- Bring water, tea, soda, coffee, etc. to the room where the family and friends are gathered.
- If children are present, try to keep them occupied so those close to the person who has died can process their emotions, make arrangements, etc.
- Do not tell children about the death unless the parents ask you to.

- Sometimes the best thing you can do is to just give the person a big hug and let her cry; there are no words that will 'make it all better.
- Remember that it is OK for you to cry and show your emotions in front of the bereaved person, but don't show more grief than appropriate. For example, don't cry and wail if the other person is quietly sobbing.

Don't . . .
- . . . make any calls or arrangements unless asked to by the next of kin.
- . . . tell anyone of the death unless you are asked to do so by the next of kin.
- . . . share any of the details of the death with anyone unless OK'd by the next of kin.
- . . . speculate on any details you do not know to be fact.

The Days Between the Death and the Funeral

What to Say
Many of the comments in the above section are appropriate for the days between the death and the funeral, also. Here are some additional suggestions that apply specifically to this time.
- *"Would you like me to help make funeral arrangements? I could call people and let them know/order flowers/go with you to the funeral home."*
- *"I will call you tomorrow/next week."* Then, make sure you do it!
- *"Can I clean your house/bring supper over/do the laundry/take the kids out for a bit?"* The grieving person may be too overwhelmed to think of something she needs done, so it's best to offer to do a specific task.
- *"It's OK to laugh/cry/scream."*
- *"It's OK to be mad at God."*

What Not to Say
- About funeral and/or memorial arrangements; *"You have to . . ." "Don't . . ." "You should not . . ."*

What to Do
- The day after the death, take food for breakfast, coffee and a coffee pot, etc., to the home where loved ones and friends are gathering. (People usually bring food for lunch and supper, but often forget breakfast.)
- Take paper plates, napkins, paper towels, toilet paper, laundry detergent, etc.—anything that will be needed in the next days and weeks when there will be many people in and out of the house.
- Call friends and neighbors to arrange for meals to be brought, help getting children to and from school and activities, housing for relatives who will be there for the funeral, and other such tasks.
- If the bereaved person goes into another room, or outside, it's OK to ask, *"Do you need company or want to be left alone?"* If she was with a group of people and then left, assume she wanted to be alone and leave her for at least a few minutes. Before you join her, ask, *"Are you ready for company or do you want to be left alone? Is there someone you want me to send to be with you?"*
- When you send a card, add a personal note instead of just signing your name. Even a brief message adds a personal touch; *"We're praying for you." "I'm thinking of you." "You are in our thoughts and prayers." "May God's comfort and peace be upon your family." "She will be missed!" "I'm so sorry!"*
- Consider adding the following Bible verses to a card or e-mail; Ps. 23, Ps. 46:1, Ps. 145:18, Is. 55:8-9, 2 Corin. 5:1-6.
- Check out websites and/or books to learn about the stages of grief and what you can do to help the grieving person. Type "death and dying" or "grief" into your search engine, or check out a book from that section in the library.

Don't . . .
- . . . make any decisions about the funeral. If a decision must be made but the person who must make it cannot, ask a close family member, pastor, or social worker to help.
- . . . try to stop the bereaved person from expressing her emotions, which may include rage and grief, by yelling, screaming, or even throwing things. These expressions of grief might make you uncomfortable, but remember this is about helping the grieving person, not your discomfort.
- . . . assume the person wants someone to be with her at all times. Some people need to be alone to rage at God, cry, or just process what has happened. If you suspect the person wants to be alone, or she tells you she does, trust that she knows what she needs. If you are afraid the person is suicidal, say; *"I know you want to be by yourself; are you planning to hurt yourself?"* If she promises she is not, leave. Ask if you can wait in another room or call her in an hour to make sure she is OK. Reassure her that she can call you at any time and you'll come back.
- . . . insist on hugging the person if she tells you not to, or pulls away or stiffens when you put your arms around her. Some people find physical touch stifles their ability to cry and grieve.
- . . . Worry too much about doing the 'wrong' or 'right' thing. Do whatever you do with love, with the goal of comforting the grieving person. Disregard your feelings of discomfort and grief, and focus on what the grieving person needs. Even if you do not do exactly what needs to be done, he or she will definitely appreciate your love and care.

At the Funeral

What to Say
- *"What a beautiful service—the music was very moving."*
- *"Look at all the flowers and plants—she touched a lot of lives."*
- *"It is OK to be sad and cry!"*
- *"We will all miss her very much!"*
- *"His death leaves a big hole in your life."*

- *"He is in heaven with Jesus now, out of pain."*

What if the deceased person's life was such that his death is almost a relief to family members and those who bore the burden of care giving? Do not tell untruths; the family members obviously know the truth. However, you can still offer comfort.
- *"The flowers and music were beautiful."*
- *"You and your family are in my prayers for comfort and peace."*

What Not to Say
- *"Don't cry—you'll ruin the funeral!"* (If you hear someone say this, you might want to tell the grieving person, *"You can call or come and see me anytime and cry!"*)

What to Do
- Pray for the family and friends to feel God's love, peace and comfort.
- Give hugs—lots of them!
- Share good memories of the person who died.

Don't . . .
- . . . bring up the appearance of the deceased person; if the loved one does, it's OK to agree or disagree with her as appropriate.
- . . . have a preconceived notion of how the loved ones of the person who died should act. They will be experiencing so many emotions and may cry, or laugh, or say nothing and show no emotion throughout the service. Remember there is no 'right' or 'wrong' way to grieve. Accept what they are feeling and doing.

In the Weeks and Months After the Death

Many people feel that after the funeral is over, they don't need to talk about the person who has died any more. The loved one may want to talk about and remember the person long after the death. You are being a true friend by offering him or her the opportunity to share memories, and continuing to offer your support long after the death.

Loved ones and friends of someone who has died will experience stages of grief for weeks, months, and even years after the death. They will have days of profound grief and days of relative normalcy. Grieving goes in cycles, not a straight line; the person may go through anger, denial, depression, back to anger, and so on, for a period of several years or even more. There is no timetable for grief; loved ones of someone who has died will probably never 'get over' the person's death.

People deal with grief in different ways. There is no one 'right' way to grieve! One person might sleep in the bed shared with a spouse the same night the person died; another person might never sleep in the bed again. One person might start sorting through and getting rid of the dead person's belongings the day after the death; another might wait years. One person might drive the deceased person's vehicle every day, while another might sell the vehicle immediately. Any and all of these reactions are normal.

Do not assume you know what 'normal' grieving is, and never presume to tell someone how they 'should grieve. No two people grieve in the same way, even if the circumstances surrounding the death of the loved one are similar. Do not expect anyone to grieve the same way you do, or the way anyone else grieves. Simply accept the person's feelings and actions while he or she goes through the process.

If you think the behaviors might be dysfunctional—for example, if the person refuses to get out of bed for several days, refuses to eat, or talks as if the loved one has not died—consult a health-care professional for guidelines as to when/if your friend needs professional help.

What to Say
- *"I don't know what to say!"* (Saying this allows the grieving person to determine the direction of the conversation; he or she may want to talk about the person who died, but also might want to talk about something else.)
- *"How are you doing today?"* (This question gives the person the option of talking about his grief if he wants to, or bringing up another subject if he does not want to. Follow his or her lead; small talk is OK!)
- *"It is OK to be sad/angry/relieved/happy."*

- *"It is OK to cry!"* (You might not be comfortable with this display of emotion, but allowing the person to express his or her emotions is part of the grieving process.)
- *"It's OK to be mad at God."*
- If the deceased person was ill for a time, you might say, *"It was a long couple of months/years when he was sick, wasn't it?"* This acknowledges a long struggle and gives the person permission to talk about the difficulties of that time.
- *"I've been through what you're going through . . . of course our situations aren't identical, but if I can help you by talking with you about it, please let me know."*
- *"What can I do for you?"*
- *"What can I do to help?"*
- *"I'd like to bring a meal over; what day is good for you?"*
- *"I will call you tomorrow/next week."* (Then, do it!)
- After a few weeks or months, when it seems appropriate; *"I have a friend who lost a loved one under similar circumstances. Would you like to talk with her?"* (Of course, ask that person if you can pass on her name before you make this offer.)
- *"I cannot take away your pain, but I can and will be here for you."*
- *"No matter what happens, I know you can handle it."*
- *"There are many people who love you and will help you get through this hard time."*
- *"God cares very much for you and your family!"*
- *"It must be hard to understand, but this is part of God's plan."*
- *"She is in heaven now, out of pain!"*

What Not to Say
- *"It's time for you to start to get over it."*
- *"You're crying too much!"*
- *"You're acting pathetic."*
- *"Don't be so sad!"*
- *"It's time to move on."*

What to Do

To provide emotional support:
- Pray for the family to feel God's love and comfort, as well as for any specific needs they may have.
- Keep the memory of the dead person alive by framing a photo for the grieving family, planting a tree in his or her memory, or setting up a memorial.
- Share memories of the person who has died. For example, *"Your grandmother encouraged me to go to college, and I always appreciated that." "Your husband had a great joke every time I saw him." "Your son was such a positive, happy boy, and I will always remember that about him."* Your comment might bring tears along with the happy memory, but that is normal.
- If you went through a similar situation, it's OK to share the feelings you had, but do not assume the other person has the same feelings. Your comments might help the other person open up about what he is feeling. Say something like, *"When my grandmother died, I felt . . . "* or, *"When my wife died, sometimes I . . . "*
- If you have had a similar loss (parent, spouse, child), tell the person that (without comparing your situations). Then, let the person talk. Remember that he needs to talk about his situation, not hear about how you are doing. It's OK to tell him if he asks, but for the most part, let him talk.
- Follow the person's lead in talking, or not talking, about the death. Some people might want to talk about it frequently while others might prefer 'business as usual' at work or in public.
- Realize that time may stand still or become skewed for the person who is grieving. She might not remember people who came by to offer sympathies, and may have mixed up the order of events following the death. If the grieving person seems not to remember something that happened, gently remind her. Review the sequence of events if she asks about it or it seems unclear to her. Remember that this is normal.
- Allow the person to cry; realize emotions can change rapidly and the person might be laughing the next minute.

- Offer to go to the cemetery with the person if she does not want to go alone.
- Send thinking-of-you cards with a brief (or long!) personal note. Share a memory of the loved one, or a Bible verse (Ps. 23, Ps. 91, Matt. 11:28-30, Rom. 15:13, Phillip. 4:19, 1 Pet. 5:7), or poem that brings you comfort.
- Continue to call, write, and visit weeks and months after the death; support after the death of a loved one can be almost overwhelming shortly after the death, but usually falls off dramatically over the following weeks and months, when it's sometimes needed the most.

Practical things to do:
- Offer to scoop snow, water plants, take animals to the vet, return library books, take the garbage to the curb, clean out the refrigerator, return medical supplies, cut the lawn, etc. Even small tasks may seem overwhelming to the grieving family.
- Invite the person out for a meal, movie, or to go shopping. This is especially important for a person who has no spouse or children living at home. Keep inviting the person to go out, even if he says *"no"* the first time (or the second, or the third).
- If the person does not seem to want to go to a public place, invite her to your home or offer to take a meal or movie to her home, and spend the evening with her.
- Remember that it is OK to admit that you do not know what to do or say.
- Offer to help sort through the deceased person's belongings and distribute them to charities, put them in storage, etc. Do not pressure the person to do this; it is normal to want to keep the loves one's things in the home for a long time after the death, just as it is normal to get rid of them shortly after the death. If the survivor wants to get rid of sentimental or significant items, suggest putting them into storage instead, in case the person wants an item in the future.
- While the family might have been overwhelmed with food immediately after the death, visitors and food offerings have probably

tapered off a few weeks after the death. Consider taking meals at this time. A take-out dinner is OK!
- Offer to pick the person up and take him or her to church, school events, or other public events normally attended with a spouse. It can be very hard to attend these events alone.
- Remember that for people mourning the loss of a loved one, tears may come at unexpected times—in church, when a favorite song is played on the radio, on holidays, at a school event, or for no apparent reason. This is normal! Accept the person's tears without judgment; offer a tissue, and a hug, or say, *"You must really be missing your dad."*
- If you inadvertently say something that causes the grieving person pain (a wife-bashing joke, for example), and then realize you've caused pain, do not say, *"Oh, I forgot you're probably still sad about that."* Do apologize by saying something like, *"I'm sorry. That was an inappropriate thing for me to say. I'm sorry for hurting you."*
- If you're seeing the person for the first time since the death, even if it is weeks or months after the death, don't ignore it. Acknowledge the death by saying, *"I was so sorry to hear of your brother's death! How are you doing?"*

Don't . . .
- . . . dwell on the subject of the death if the person wants to talk about something else.
- . . . try to change the subject if the person does want to talk about the death or the person who died.
- . . . avoid saying the deceased person's name; it's OK to talk about him or her even if it brings tears.
- . . . avoid talking about the dead person, or about the subject of death. Talking about it might bring tears, but tears are a part of healing and acceptance.
- . . . avoid the person when you see him in public. It happens often, and grieving people say it is very difficult when they can tell someone is avoiding them. When you see the grieving person, overcome your discomfort and express your sympathy.

- ... assume that if the person doesn't talk about visiting the cemetery or show outward signs of grief, he or she is not grieving. Some people are more open about their grief while others prefer to keep it private.
- ... project your feelings of how you think someone should grieve, onto the grieving person. It's OK to be concerned if you think the grieving is abnormal, but before you try to change how the person is expressing his grief, talk with a health-care professional who can tell you if the grieving is normal or in fact you do need to take some kind of action.
- ... ask a person if they will be moving, selling their house, or making any big life changes. It is insensitive to suggest such a big change after such an already traumatic event, and experts say one should not make any major changes for at least a year after the death of a loved one.

When You are Grieving

What to Say
In most cases, the only response you need to give is one of the following:
- *"Thank you."*
- *"I appreciate your thoughts and prayers."*
- *"Please pray for _____"*
- *"We will miss her very, very much."*

If someone makes an inappropriate or hurtful comment, it is probably because he or she did not know what to say, but wanted to say something. Most times it's best just to take the comment in the spirit in which it was intended and reply, *"Thank you."* However, if you have heard the same hurtful remark several times from the same person, it's OK to draw his attention to it by saying something like,
- *"I know you care and I thank you for that. It helps me when you let me grieve and heal in the way I need to, even if it's not how you would."*
- *"Everyone grieves at their own pace. I'm not ready to give away her clothes yet."*

- *"I need to cry; my tears are part of the healing process. I'm sorry it makes you uncomfortable when I cry. All you have to do is give me a hug."*
- If someone keeps telling you that you are grieving in the 'wrong' way, you might need to make your comeback a little stronger; *"This is my way of grieving; please do not tell me to do it differently. What I'm doing is normal." "I'm sorry you don't think I'm doing this right; it's the first time I've had a husband die."*

What Not to Say
- *"Um, er, do you think you could maybe please, not tell me you don't like what I'm doing and how I'm grieving?"* (It is OK to be firm with your request.)

What to Do
- If you prefer not to be hugged or touched when you are crying, gently say, *"Please don't touch me when I'm crying; it makes it harder to express my emotions. I know you mean well, but I'm one of the people who is uncomfortable with that touch. Just sit here close."*
- You might want to be alone after the death for a time to rage at God, or cry, or just think with no one around. Well-meaning friends and family will probably want to remain at your side. Again, be gentle with them, and reassuring; *"I need to be alone to process all of this. It's OK that you leave; I will not hurt myself. You can call me in an hour to make sure I'm OK, but for now, please let me have some times alone."*
- Tell people what they can do to help. It's a blessing to them, when you allow them to help you.

Don't . . .
- . . . allow anyone to criticize how you grieve. If someone does this, explain and insist that you be allowed to grieve in the way that is right for you.

When Someone is Dying

It can be difficult to spend time with someone who is dying, but it is also a great privilege to share this time with them. During their last months, days, and hours, most people want and need the presence friends who are caring, compassionate, and will listen.

To the Person Who is Dying

What to Say
- *"What are your last wishes?" "What can I do for you?" "Is there anyone you want to see, or anything you want to do? How can I help that to happen?"*

After you receive the answers, grant the requests to the best of your ability, and/or find someone who can. The requests might be as simple as savoring a bowl of ice cream or hearing you read his favorite poems, or as profound as apologizing to someone for a long-ago misunderstanding or reconciling with a loved one. If a special someone cannot be there in person, perhaps they can talk by phone. Often there are unresolved issues that need to be resolved, both for the benefit of the person who is living, and the one who is dying. When you facilitate a last request, you are giving a great gift.
- *"Who is to make medical decisions if you are no longer able to?"*
  It is vital that the dying person's wishes be known by someone legally appointed to carry them out.
- *"Would you like me to pray with you?" "May I pray for you?"*
  Ask this even if you're not sure of the person's beliefs or know he is not a believer. She may be ready to hear about salvation, and you could be the one to lead her to Christ!
- If you are not comfortable praying out loud, you might want to say something like, *"You are in my thoughts and prayers. Is there something specific you would like me to pray for, for you?"*
- *"I am here with you."*
- *"You are not alone; God is with you and always will be."*

What Not to Say
- *"Don't say things like that." "Don't feel that way."* Someone who is dying does not have the luxury of time or energy for pretending things are not as they are. Allow the person to share his or her feelings, even if you are not comfortable hearing them.

What to Do
- If the person's wishes regarding health care are not legally recorded (in a living will or advanced health care directive), encourage her to discuss this with relatives.
- Recall your times together; it's OK to laugh!
- Tell the person you love, admire, and value her. Leave nothing unsaid that you want the person to know before she dies.
- If you have not shared your faith in God with the person, but wish to do so, here is a way to start that conversation. *"We've been friends for a long time, but I feel bad for not having talked to you about something that is very important in my life—my faith in and relationship with God. He wants us all to be with Him in heaven when we die. Even if you did not know Him through your life, it is never too late. He wants you! Can I tell you more?"* If the person says *"No,"* say, *"Please think about it. You can do it on your own, and it's never too late. God loves you and wants to spend eternity with you, no matter what you've done or not done during your life."*
- If the person wants to hear more, continue with, *"To accept the Lord and receive the gift of heaven, all you have to do is admit that you have sinned and believe that Jesus died for your sins, and rose from the dead. Would you like to confess and accept Him as your Savior?"* If the person has questions that you are uncomfortable answering, call a chaplain to answer the questions. If the person is unable to verbally answer, he can just squeeze your hand to signal acceptance.
- Leave a selection of Bible verses, written out (Ps. 145:18, Ps. 46:1, Matt. 11:28-30, John 3:16, Rom. 1:9-10), for the person to read later.
- A dying person may choose his or her time to die. This could be after they have seen a special person one more time, or made

amends for something hurtful that happened. Sometimes a person will wait until someone has left the room, to let go and die; another person might wait for the arrival of someone and die shortly thereafter. If you sense the person is hanging on, you might want to say something like, *"I love you and I'll miss you. I will never, ever forget you! Do what you need to do, when you are ready." "We will miss you and never forget you; we will be OK when you are gone." "I know you are dying . . . it is OK to go when you are ready."*
- Be positive; note good things like the nice weather, the person having a good day, or issues that have been resolved. However, remain realistic; don't ignore the dying process.
- Call before you visit to see if it's a good time to visit, and ask if the patient or caregivers need anything that you can take.
- Remember that a person who is in a coma or appears to be unresponsive may still be aware of what is happening around him, and may be able to hear what is being said in the room. Do not say anything at the bedside that you would not say if you knew the person could hear you. Talk to the person as you would if you he could respond.
- Small talk is OK; mention the weather, tell a joke, talk about what you've been doing, mention nurses and doctors or friends and family members coming into and leaving the room. Tell him who is present in the room, especially if he has been waiting for someone specific to arrive.
- Share memories of his life.
- Tell him or her anything you want to, before he or she dies.
- Read Bible verses; for example, Ps. 23:4, Ps. 145:18, or Matt. 11:28-30.
- Pray out loud if you are comfortable doing so.

Don't . . .
- . . . try to pretend that the person is not dying.
- . . . be unrealistic by insisting the person will live to see a far-off event.
- . . . allow your discomfort to get in the way of communicating openly with the person and sharing special moments together.

- ... be afraid to talk about death, even if it makes you uncomfortable.

To Someone Whose Loved One is Dying
Your friend needs your support when her loved one is dying, whether it's after a long illness or is sudden, after an accident or brief illness. Regardless of whether she's had months or minutes to prepare for the death, she needs your support.

What to Say
- *"I'm so sorry!"*
- *"What can I do for you?"*
- *"How is he today?"*
- *"He looks comfortable."*
- *"Is there anything he or she needs, that I can get for you on my way to the hospital?"*
- *"What should I ask for in my prayers?"*
- *"Is there anyone you would like me to call?"*

What Not to Say
- Regarding medical decisions; *"You should . . ."* *"You should not . . ."*
- *"It will be just fine," "He will come out of it,"* if the person clearly will not recover.

What to Do
- Encourage your friend to talk with her loved one and to make sure nothing is left unsaid.
- Offer to stay with the dying person so your friend can take a break.
- Reassure your friend that she is making the right decisions regarding the loved one who is dying.
- Ask medical professionals what to expect, and how you can support your friend.
- Ask your friend if she has questions, and if so, get answers from the medical professionals.

- Recite or send a card or e-mail with the following verses; 2 Cor. 5:1-7, Phillip. 4:19, 1 Pet. 5:7.

Don't ...
- ... ignore the impending death.
- ... question or criticize any decisions your friend makes, medical or otherwise.

Suicide

Suicide accounted for more than 32,000 deaths in 2004. Another 8-25 people attempted to die by suicide for every person who did die by suicide in 2004 and approximately 400,000 people were treated in an Emergency Room or hospitalized for self-inflicted injuries in 2002. You can see from these numbers that many people are touched by friends or family attempting, or succeeding at, death by suicide every year.

If Someone Threatens Suicide
It's chilling to hear someone say they're thinking of committing suicide. Our natural first response is to tell the person not to feel that way, and change the subject. However, if someone tells you he is considering suicide, he trusts you, and at that moment, wants help. It is vitally important to take any and all suicide threats seriously.

You must conquer your feelings of fear and dread and help the person through this time.

What to Say
- If someone makes comments like, *"It's all too much for me," "It's not worth living anymore," "They would be better off without me," "I wish it would all just end," "I just can't go on anymore," "I want to die,"* realize that this is a sign that someone is considering attempting suicide and a cry for help. (Other signs include, prolonged sadness and depression, expressions of hopelessness, writing notes or poems about death or suicide, excessive guilt or shame, facing a situation he perceives

as humiliating, feeling like a failure, giving away prized possessions, purchasing a weapon.) If someone makes comments like this, ask him, *"Are you thinking of hurting yourself?"* You will *not* put the idea of suicide in someone's mind if you bring it up. Instead, you are offering the person the opportunity to share his feelings.

If the person replies that he is thinking of hurting himself, ask,
- *"What are you thinking of doing?" "Do you have a plan?"* If the person has a plan, see the "What to Do" section below.

Even if the person says he does not have a plan, he is still in danger of hurting himself. Say,
- *"There is hope, and there are many reasons to go on."*
- *"I feel bad that you feel so very bad about your life; I think talking with a psychiatrist/counselor/pastor would help. Would you like me to make an appointment? I'll go with you if you want me to."* It's best if the person sees a psychiatrist, but talking with anyone is preferable to talking with only non-professionals.
- *"It's going to be OK; I am here for you and will be here with you through this time."*
- *"You are important to me!"*
- *"I love you!"*
- *"God loves you no matter what happened or what you did."*

What Not to Say
- *"Oh, don't say that."*
- *"You don't really mean it."*
- *"It's not that bad!"*
- *"You wouldn't do that."*
- *"Get over it."*
- *"Toughen up; it's not that bad!"*
- *"Everything will turn out just fine. Don't worry!"*

What to Do

Obviously, a person who is has suicidal thoughts and/or a plan to die by suicide, needs professional mental health help. Take the following actions, depending on the exact circumstances;

- Pray for guidance as to what to say and do, and for the person to feel God's love and peace (even if he or she is not a believer).
- Realize that a kind word or action can make a huge difference to someone who is depressed or suicidal. Your words or actions do not have to be profound, just caring and sincere.
- If the person has a concrete plan to die by suicide, the situation is dire. If you are with the person, do not leave him! If you are not with him, immediately contact a friend or loved one to stay with that person until someone else is there to stay, you've gotten the person to a hospital, or you are absolutely convinced he is not going to hurt himself. If you can't reach someone, call 911 to report the situation and request someone to go stay with the person.
- If the person is suicidal when you are there, take him to the emergency room and insist that he be seen by a psychiatrist, or be transferred to a facility where a psychiatrist is available. This is essential even if the person is no longer suicidal by the time he gets to the hospital.
- Contact the person's spouse, parents, adult children, and/or other adults who love and will help the person get the help he needs. Do not leave a suicidal person alone.
- Arrange for the care of any children in the home. Do not leave a very depressed or suicidal parent alone with his or her minor age children, especially if they are very young.
- Call the person's doctor, counselor, psychiatrist, or a clergy person. If necessary, make an appointment for the person and accompany him to the appointment. Make sure he is not left alone until the appointment, or promises not to hurt himself (or says he is no longer thinking of hurting himself and promises to call someone if he feels like hurting himself).
- Let the person talk as much as he wants to; listen closely for details of why he's feeling so much pain as to consider death by suicide.

- Allow the person to cry, talk, yell, and so on, to express his emotions.
- If the person's response to, *"Do you have a plan?"* is *"No,"* ask why he said he was thinking of hurting himself. Obviously, thoughts about suicide are very serious, even if he does not have a plan.
- Be an advocate for the person; go to doctor appointments with him, call doctors, counselors, psychiatrists, hospitals, and so on, until the person gets the help he or she needs.
- Offer the person the hope that help is available, and that there are alternatives to suicide—debts can be paid off, there are treatments for almost every medical problem, families may reconcile, problems can be worked through.
- Assure the person that you are concerned and care about him.
- Remain calm and non judgmental, as difficult as that may be!
- Tell friends and family members who will be supportive, about the person's threats. Educate them on the warning signs of suicide, what you've been doing to help, what the person has been threatening, etc. Enlist their help in getting the person professional help.
- Ask the person to promise to call you, another friend or family member, psychiatrist, pastor, etc., if the suicidal feelings return.
- Take suicide threats seriously, even if the person has made them before. Continue to insist that the person get the help he or she needs.
- Reassure the person of God's unconditional love.

Don't . . .
- . . . discount a person's suicidal feelings, or think that *"if he says he will, he really won't attempt to die by suicide."*
- . . . say nothing if you sense or know someone is depressed or suspect he or she may be considering suicide; a kind word or deed can give someone the will to *not* attempt suicide.
- . . . label the person's feelings and/or thoughts as 'good' or 'bad.'
- . . . act shocked; your reaction might cause the person to withdraw and not talk with you.
- . . . dare someone to attempt to die by suicide.

- ... promise not to tell anyone; it is imperative that others know of the suicidal thoughts, either directly from the person having the thoughts, or through you.

If a person attempts, or succeeds at dying by suicide, survivors may feel extremely guilty, whether or not they knew of the person's thoughts and intentions. Remember that some people exhibit no signs that they are planning to die by suicide, and other people, regardless of the steps taken by family, friends, and professionals, succeed at dying by suicide.

If you are involved in a situation where someone close to you attempts or dies by suicide, consider talking with a healthcare professional to cope with your feelings.

When Someone Dies by Suicide

When someone dies by suicide, the loved ones left behind may have many questions, and experience a wide range of emotions, including sadness, anger, guilt, relief, blame. Comfort them as you would anyone else who has experienced the death a loved one. (For more suggestions of what to say and do after the death of a loved one, see the sections on death earlier in this chapter).

What to Say
- *"I am so very, very sorry!"*
- *"How are you doing?"* (Of course the answer to this is, *"Not very well at all,"* but you are giving the person a chance to express his feelings.)
- *"Do you want to tell me about it?"* (This conveys your acceptance of the surviving person, as well as the circumstances surrounding the death.)
- *"We went through this when our child/a friend/parent died by suicide . . . If it would help you to hear how we made it through that time, please let us know."*

- "God is with you . . . " "I wish you God's comfort and peace."
- "It is OK to be mad at God."

What Not to Say
- "*I saw it coming!*"/"*Didn't you see this coming?*" (Sometimes it is just not possible to see any signs or prevent death by suicide.)
- "God needed another child in heaven."
- "Where did he/she get the knife/pills/rope?"
- "I don't want to mention him because it might make you cry."
- "Why did he do it?"
- "Doesn't talking about it just bring it all back?" (Loved ones never forget.)
- "He's at peace."
- "He's in a better place now." (To loved ones, there was nothing wrong with the place he was at, here with them.)
- "You're still young enough to have more children." "At least you have other kids." (Every child is unique and no child can take the place of another!)
- "You'll have to get over it sooner or later."
- "It's better for everyone this way."
- "Be glad he killed himself before he killed you or someone else."
- "I thought you were such a nice, normal family!"
- "Time heals all wounds."
- "I know just exactly how you feel."
- "You need to forgive yourself." (This comment implies the survivor did something wrong.)
- "My son was acting up, but I saw the signs and knew what to do; I had him admitted to a psych ward so he was safe."
- "I guess your child did not go to heaven."
- "Do you think there was something you could have done to prevent it?"
- "Suicide is the coward's way out."
- "Maybe you could get a dog." (Nothing will ever take the place of the loved one!)

What to Do
- Accept his or her emotions and feelings of grief, anger, sadness, guilt. You do not have to give answers—no one can do that—but reassure the person that her feelings are normal and just listen.

Don't ...
- ... speculate on the possibility of suicide if the circumstances of death are not clear.
- ... speculate on the reasons for the suicide.
- ... become excessively emotional if you accidentally use a phrase like *"hang in there,"* or *"I'd just shoot myself,"* and the person's loved one died by hanging or shooting himself. Loved ones understand accidental references to the suicide and will become more upset if you become overly upset.
- ... avoid talking about the fact that the person died by suicide; talking about how the person died is a necessary part of the grieving process.

(for suggestions on what to say to and do for—and not say and do—someone who has attempted suicide, see Chapter 7, the section Various Sticky, Tricky, Uncomfortable Situations.)

Miscarriage

Around 20% of pregnancies end in miscarriage, so chances are great someone you know has, or will, experience a miscarriage. When someone suffers a miscarriage the loss is real, even if there was no outward evidence of the baby. The parents, as well as siblings, grandparents, and other relatives, suffer the loss of hopes and dreams about a baby who now will not be born. Here are some suggestions for comforting someone who has experienced that loss.

What to Say
- *"I'm so very sorry for your loss!"*
- *"How are you feeling?"* (This allows the woman to talk about her physical, as well as emotional, feelings.)

- "*I cannot imagine the pain and loss you must be feeling!*"
- "*It's OK to be mad at God.*"
- "*I've experienced miscarriages; it was a very painful time. If I can help you by telling you about it, please let me know.*"
- "*We lost a baby several years ago. Maybe our babies are playing together in heaven.*"
- "*What a great loss! I'm praying for your peace and for God to give you comfort and peace and continued direction in your life.*"

What Not to Say
- "*It wasn't really a baby, just a bunch of cells. Don't be so sad.*"
- "*It must have been deformed.*"
- "*It just wasn't mean to be.*" (If the other person says this, it's OK to agree with her.)
- "*At least you have your other children.*" (Babies are not interchangeable!)
- "*You might not have been a good parent anyway.*"
- "*You won't miss what you never had.*"
- "*You can have my children!*"
- "*Do you want to hold my baby?*"
- "*You're not missing much; kids are so much trouble.*"
- "*At least you didn't get attached to the baby.*"
- "*I just know God will give you your miracle baby.*" (No, you do not know that!)
- "*It's God's will—accept it and move on.*"
- "*You can try again.*" "*You'll get pregnant again soon.*" "*You'll have a healthy baby someday.*" (Many women are not able to conceive after a miscarriage, or have multiple miscarriages.)

What to Do
The general suggestions about what to do after a death, earlier in the chapter, are appropriate, as well as the following.
- Acknowledge the loss as you would any other death; with cards, flowers, and memorials.
- If you have experienced a miscarriage, say something like, "*I lost a baby, too, and it was very hard!*" Don't go into the details

unless the other person asks; this is not about your experience, but about sympathizing with the person who has just recently experienced the loss.
- Remember that the father, grandparents and siblings are feeling the loss, too! Express your sympathies to them. CAUTION: Make sure extended family members were aware of the pregnancy before mentioning the miscarriage; the parents might not have shared the news of the pregnancy with all family members.
- Remember that as well as the emotional loss, the mother is experiencing the physical manifestations of miscarriage; hormonal and physical changes, and possibly a surgical procedure. Offer to take a meal, clean her house, watch her kids, go shopping for groceries, and so on, so she can begin to heal physically as well as emotionally.
- Accept and encourage any rituals that the parents choose, to help them remember the baby. They might want to make footprints, and/or have a memorial service or burial.
- Ask the parents how they are doing weeks and months later (especially around the baby's due date), not just immediately after the miscarriage.
- Remember that it takes time to grieve this loss of a baby; it does not take less time to recover from the death of an unborn baby, than the death of an adult loved one.
- Realize that a person who has had a miscarriage may cry when she sees a diaper commercial, a baby, or attends a baby shower.
- Send a card or e-mail; consider including a verse like Psalm 18:30, Pro. 3:5-6, or Matt. 14:19.

Don't...
- ...ask for the baby furniture or any supplies purchased for the baby who died.
- ...clean out the nursery for them; doing that is part of the healing process. It is OK to help if you're asked.
- ...discount the grieving process just because the baby had not been born.

Death of a Full-Term Baby, or Child

The loss of a baby or child is devastating, regardless of the age of the child or circumstances surrounding the death.

All of the things listed earlier in this chapter are appropriate to say and do, and not say and do, in the event of the death of a baby or child. Here are some additional comments specific to this situation.

What to Say
- *"We lost a child, too; he was just three. I know at least a little of what you are going through."*
- *"We have an angel in heaven, too. Our first baby died shortly after he was born."* *"Maybe our babies are playing together in heaven!"*
- *"Do you want to tell me about it?"* *"Do you mind if I ask a question? If it's too painful, you don't have to answer."* (Sometimes part of healing involves recounting the accident, illness, or circumstances surrounding the death, over and over. It might be hard to listen, but remember that your listening is helping your friend through the grieving process.)

What Not to Say
- *"At least you have other children,"* or, *"You can always have another child."* (Babies and children are not interchangeable!)
- *"He's better off now."* (This implies the loved ones should not be grieving. Even though believers know that their child is in heaven, they're still devastated over the loss.)

What to Do
- Pray for God's peace and comfort for your friends. Pray that you will be led to say the right words.
- Some parents, moms especially, experience a loss of memory, or distortion of time, of the events surrounding the death. They might not remember people who visited them at the hospital or at home, or who sent flowers or brought food or even attended the funeral. If she comments that no one visited her at the hospital and you know otherwise, gently remind her of that, and don't

take it personally if she doesn't remember your caring gestures. Because she might not recall your gestures of caring and support, be sure to call, write, and/or visit frequently.
- Help with the other children; take them to school, shopping for funeral clothes if necessary, to the park so the parents have some time to themselves.
- Allow the parents to relive the tragedy as many times as they want, as hard as it is to hear. Accept the person's emotions and feelings.
- Offer to return baby items or medical supplies that will not be used, or offer to go with the person who returns them.

Don't...
- ... be afraid to talk about the child, and cry with the parents.
- ... ask for baby clothes or furniture *"since you won't be using it now."*
- ... pressure the parents to attend baby showers or hold a baby, look at ultrasound pictures, etc.

Anniversaries, Holidays, Birthdays, and Special Occasions after the Death of a Loved One

Realize that things will not be 'normal' for the people close to the person who has died, for a very long time. It may be several years, or even longer, before someone emerges from the fog of losing a loved one. The first Christmas, birthday, wedding anniversary, Father's or Mother's Day, and so on, will bring many emotions, as will the date of birth and death of the person who has died. These landmark days will never be the same, and it will take several years, at least, to develop new routines and traditions and ways of celebrating without the loved one who died.

The loved ones left behind will always remember special days, and you will not be reminding him of something he'd forgotten when you mention the significance of the day. Your comments may evoke tears or sadness, but you are giving a gift by allowing the person to cry, share memories, or just talk about the person who is not present.

There may be sad moments on landmark days like weddings, graduations, or the birth of a child, when someone who has died, is acutely missed.

Other deaths (that of a child or spouse of a close friend, or a relative suffering a miscarriage) might bring back the memories of similar events your friend experienced when her own child or spouse died. Be prepared for your friend to experience more intense feelings of grief at this time. If she does not realize why she's especially sad, suggest that the other death is reminding her of her own loss.

The anniversary of a miscarriage will be remembered, as will the date the baby was due to be born. After a child's death, parents will remember him on landmark days like the first day of school each year, when his class is confirmed or graduates, and other significant events the child would have been a part of.

Some people find the days leading up to an anniversary or holiday more difficult, emotionally, than the actual date itself. For others, the days after might be more difficult. Do not expect the person to act a certain way on or around these significant dates. He might want to spend the day privately, just with family members, or with a group of people. He might want to follow long-held traditions to commemorate a holiday, birthday, or anniversary, or start new traditions. Neither one is wrong.

Your phone call, e-mail, card, or visit on days surrounding the date, not just the date itself, will help your friend.

Here are some things you can say and do to show your support.

When Someone is Facing a Significant Date after the Death of a Loved One

What to Say
- *"I just wanted to tell you I'm thinking of you today."* (This opens the conversation so the person can talk about the loved one if he wants to.)
- *"I was thinking about Grandma today, and how much I miss her."*

- "It would have been your son's birthday today, so I've been thinking about him. How are you doing?"
- "I know next week is the anniversary of your husband's death. Are you going to the cemetery? Would you like me to go with you?"
- "I remember that you and your wife used to celebrate Valentine's Day, which is next week. Would you like some company on that day?"
- "It's OK to be sad. I know you miss her even after all these years."
- "He would have loved to have been at his daughter's wedding."

What Not to Say
- "It's been two years, and should be getting easier. Why are you still so upset?"
- "Don't even think about it being his birthday; you'll only be sad."
- "It's time for you to just get over it."

What to Do
- Pray for your friend to be comforted with memories of the loved one, and that he or she will feel God's comfort and peace.
- Remember the person on the significant date, or several days before or after, with a thinking-of-you card, phone call, or e-mail. Mention the significance of the date and follow the person's lead in talking about (or not talking about) the person who has died.
- Support the person in whatever way he chooses to spend the day.
- Consider continuing a tradition; if the deceased husband and his wife traditionally watched a special movie together on their anniversary, ask her if she'd like you to rent that movie and watch it with her.
- Many times a parent who has died is remembered at a child's wedding with a special flower, dance, or mention in the program. Use this as an opening to bring up the person who is not present. It might bring tears, but the family members are missing the person whether you mention him or not, and your bringing up

the subject allows them to share their feelings and is part of the healing process. You might say something like, *"The only thing that would make this better is if your mom would have been here. She would have loved it." "It's neat that you remembered your dad with that flower arrangement. He would have loved being here!"*

Don't . . .
- . . . have a preconceived notion of how the person should spend the day, or act.
- . . . ignore the date, thinking you'll only make your friend sad by remembering it. He or she is certainly thinking about the person who is not there to celebrate!

When You are Facing a Significant Date Without a Loved One

Some people will forget dates that are significant to you (or not realize their importance), after you've lost a loved one. Some people might hesitate to bring it up, for fear of reminding you about it. If you want to talk about your loved one, here are some suggestions for getting the support you need.

What to Say
- *"I'm really missing my husband today. Can I come over?"*
- *"It's nice to talk about her with someone, even if it makes me cry."*
- *"It makes me cry to think of her, but it's nice to hear your memories."*
- *"Next week is our anniversary and I don't want to be alone that day. Would you like to go shopping and to a movie?"*
- *"Thanks for asking me to join you for Thanksgiving, but I think I want to be alone that day."*
- *"Our son's birthday is tomorrow. I'm going to go to the cemetery; would you come with me?"*

What Not to Say
- *"I can't believe you forgot that this was her birthday."*

What to Do
- Bring up the significance of the date—others may hesitate to do so.
- Reach out to a friend, your pastor or priest, or a counselor, if you need someone to talk with on significant dates.

Don't . . .
- . . . assume people don't care if they don't remember, or don't bring up the significance of a special day.

Death of a Pet

Do not minimize the death of a pet! Many children grow up with pets, and many people get a pet when they're going through a difficult time in their lives. There can be deep emotional bonds between pets and family members, and pets are a part of many happy family memories.

What to Say
- *"What happened?"*
- *"I did not know your horse, but would you like to tell me about her?"*
- *"Your dog was with you through many hard times in your life. You will really miss her."*
- *"He was part of your family for a long time!"*
- *"How long was he in your family?"*
- *"I know how much you all loved him."*
- *"Your cat had so much personality—she licked me and jumped on me every time I visited."*
- *"I'm so sorry he died."*

What Not to Say
- *"It was just a pet—get over it."*
- *"You can get another one; there are plenty of cats around."*
- *"What are you so upset about? It was just a dog."*
- *"It's not like you lost a human loved one."*

What to Do
- Call to express your sympathy; call several weeks later also.
- Send a sympathy card (some are made for pets!) or thinking-of-you card.
- Accept the owner's decisions about medical treatment, euthanasia, burial of the pet, etc.
- Recognize that a pet *is* a family member, especially if the couple has no children.
- Make a memory box and fill it with mementos of the pet; perhaps a lock of hair, any awards ribbons a show pet has won, pictures of family members with the pet, a sample of his or her pet food, a toy. Give it to the family at a time that seems appropriate.

Don't . . .
- . . . surprise them with another pet.
- . . . trivialize or minimize the death of the pet.

Chapter 6

Illness, Injury, and Disability

A serious illness or injury causes major life disruptions for the person who is sick or hurt, as well as his or her friends and family. Your kind words and deeds can make getting through this difficult time easier.

Acute (Short) Illness or Injury

To the Ill or Injured Person

What to Say
- *"You are in my thoughts and prayers."*
- *"God is watching over you!"*
- *"What happened?"* (Asking in this way lets the person answer as briefly or in as much detail as he or she wants to.)
- *"I'm sorry this happened."*
- *"How are you doing today?"*
- *"It happened so suddenly!"*
- *"Your wife said you're doing better today."*
- *"Many people are concerned and wishing you a speedy recovery."*

Small talk is OK;
- *"It's raining outside today, and it's supposed to turn to snow later."*
- *"Your daughters are still here; I offered to stay with you while they get something to eat. "*

What Not to Say
- *"It couldn't have been worse than childbirth!"* (This minimizes the pain the person is in.)
- *"You are so lucky it wasn't worse!"* (The person who is hurt or ill might not feel lucky.)
- *"Tell them to do more tests and find out what's really wrong."*
- *"My father was out of the hospital three days after his surgery; you will be too."* (Everyone's experience is different.)
- *"You'll be up and around in no time!" "I just know you'll be as good as new very soon."* (Do not make predictions about the person's recovery.)
- *"Have the doctor prescribe _____ (medication). It worked for me!"* (Every case is different; just because a medication worked for you (or someone you know) does not mean it will for the person you're talking to.)

What to Do
- Pray for the person's recovery and for him to accept God's will regarding the extent and course of his recovery.
- Remember that even someone who is unresponsive may be able to hear you; talk to him even if he cannot respond. Read the person the cards at his bedside, reassure him that he is being well cared for. Small talk (about the weather, hometown events) is fine!
- Be realistic about the person's condition; do not tell him he will be recovered in 'no time' if that is clearly not true.
- Send a card or e-mail; include one of the following verses; Ps. 23, Ps. 91, Heb. 13:5b-6, Phillip. 4:19, 1 Pet. 5:7.

Don't ...
- ... make any negative comments about the ill or injured person or his condition.
- ... make predictions about the person's recovery.
- ... comment on treatments, surgeries, medical care, medications, etc. unless you are an experienced, qualified, medical professional, and know all the details of the illness or injury. Every case is different. Do not assume that since someone you know in a similar situation received certain care, another person's treatment or recovery will take the same path.
- ... talk about someone else's experiences with an accident or illness (other than very briefly, in generalities); doing so diminishes what the ill or injured person is going through.
- ... send flowers if someone in in the Intensive Care Unit; they may not be allowed in patient rooms. Some hospitals do not allow latex balloons, either.

To the Spouse/Close Relatives

The spouse and close relatives of the sick or injured person will be under great stress and may have many feelings, perhaps conflicting, as a result of the sudden and dramatic changes in the life of their loved one, as well as the changes in their own lives and concerns about the future. The spouse or other close relatives will be making many decisions, some of them difficult, related to medical care, finances, and living arrangements.

What to Say

While you should not make specific comments/suggestions about a person's medical care, it is OK to make general comments like,
- *"He looks better today!"*
- *"She looks very comfortable."*
- *"This hospital has a very good reputation for dealing with this type of illness."*
- *"The nurses are very attentive and kind."*
- *"How is he doing today?"*
- *"What should we pray for, for you and your family?"*

- *"I spent days in the hospital after my father-in-law had his accident, so I can relate to what you're going through."*
- *"What would you like me to tell people who are asking about him?"* (then she can pass on details she wants made public).
- *"Are there some calls I can make for you?"* (perhaps to her employer, to update friends or relatives, make arrangements for babysitting kids at home, etc.).
- *"What can I do to help you? Would you like something to eat? Coffee? A change of clothes?"*
- *"It's OK to cry/be sad/mad/upset/take a break."*
- *"How are you doing?"*

What Not to Say
- *"Your doctor should prescribe _____ (medication). That's what my mother was on and it worked great." "Tell the doctor to do ____ (test/procedure)."* (Unless you know all the details of the case, and are a medical professional, do not offer medical advice. You increase the stress and confusion of loved ones when you questions the doctors, nurses, or treatment.)
- *"Are you sure you have the best doctors?"*
- Anything negative, like, *"I read once that 90% of patients that are as sick as he is will die,"* or, *"He will have a very long and very hard recovery."*

What to Do
- After you visit someone who is ill or injured, be very careful about passing on information about his condition. It is almost impossible to get a true picture of his condition (which could quickly and frequently change) from a brief visit. If you pass on inaccurate information, a family member must correct it later, adding to their stress. It's also distressing for family members to hear inaccurate information about how 'good' their loved one is doing, when the person is not doing that well. Ask a family member, who is best able to give you an accurate account of the patient's condition, what to tell other people if they ask. Otherwise, give general answers like: *"We were just there for a few minutes, but he ate all of his lunch." "We couldn't tell*

very much from such a brief visit. His wife said he is slowly improving, but there are setbacks too."
- Allow the person to be discouraged; if you say, *"After my dad's surgery, he had setbacks like your dad is having, and I remember being very discouraged for a time,"* or, *"It's hard when her condition changes so rapidly, isn't it,"* you're allowing the person to share the negative emotions he or she may be experiencing.
- Offer realistic encouragement; *"My sister was in very serious condition after her accident, but she recovered,"* or, *"He was in very good shape before he got sick, and that will help him recover."*
- Remember that the spouse and close relatives are under a great deal of stress. They are probably asked the same questions about their loved one several times a day, and they are probably not sleeping or eating well. Do not be surprised if they are moody or short tempered, and do not take it personally!
- Ask the spouse/loved ones how they are doing, and remind them to take care of themselves by eating and resting. The person might be overwhelmed and not know how to take care of herself, so offer to bring lunch, coffee, snacks, and/or stay at the bedside of her loved one so she can get some rest or take a shower. The person might get tired of being reminded to take care of herself, so if she answers your questions very briefly, or makes comments like, *"I'm tired of talking about it,"* talk about something else instead, perhaps the weather or what's happening in your family (small talk is OK).
- On the other hand, if the condition of the ill or injured person is not life threatening, or has been stable, loved ones might not get asked how they're doing, although they still need to know they're cared about.
- Remember that the person is under great stress and the next time you talk or visit, might not remember what you talked about during the previous visit.
- Listen and accept all emotions expressed—sorrow, guilt, anger, relief. Allow the person to cry, laugh, or be mad at God.
- Offer a hug.
- If the caregiver will be spending days or weeks at the hospital, ask what he or she needs. Bring snacks, microwaveable meals,

gift cards to nearby restaurants or stores, a newspaper, a portable CD player, a devotion book. Remember it will be hard for her to concentrate so don't bring a novel or complicated puzzle book unless she asks.
- Prepare a care package with favorite snacks, a toothbrush and paste, cards for her, lotion, photographs of people she loves, and other comfort items.
- Send a card or e-mail, perhaps containing one of the following appropriate verses; Matt. 11:28-30, 2 Cor. 9:8, 1 Pet. 5:7, Heb. 13:5b-6.
- Invite her out to lunch, or offer to sit with her loved one while she gets out for a few minutes, or a few hours.
- Be specific with your offers of help; for example, offer to check the caregiver's home—feed pets, water plants, get the mail, and so on.
- Offer to be the key contact person who e-mails or calls family and friends with updates on the person's condition. This will cut down drastically on the number of phone calls the loved one has to answer.
- Sit in silence; use the caregiver's behavior (talking, crying, reaching out) to guide yours.
- Offer to take care of the kids, be at her home when hospital equipment is delivered, restock the refrigerator before they return home, or other big favors that the person might be reluctant to ask for.

Don't ...
- ... make predictions about the person's course of recovery.
- ... have a preconceived notion of how the spouse of an injured or ill person 'should' act, or what her response to news of the loved one's condition 'should' be. She is probably experiencing a mix of feelings and emotions, depending on the circumstances surrounding the accident/injury, her previous relationship with the hospitalized person, and an uncertain outcome. Accept what he/she is feeling.
- ... offer your medical opinion about medical tests, medications, diagnosis or treatment, unless you are a trained medical profes-

sional. Every case is different and treatment is based on many, many variables. Trying to second guess the medical professionals just adds more stress, especially if the diagnosis and/or treatment is tricky.

During a Lengthy Recovery, at Home or in the Hospital

To the Person Who Is Ill or Injured

What to Say
- *"How are you today?"*
- *"It is OK to be sad/discouraged/angry/happy."*
- *"I would like to visit tomorrow afternoon; would that be a good time? Can I bring you a book or a movie?"*
- *"This long recovery must be frustrating sometimes."* (When you say this, you allow the person to talk about his feelings, even if they are negative at that time.)
- *"God is with you every step of the way."*

What Not to Say
- *"It's sure taking you a long time to get better!"*
- *"Why is it taking you so long to get over it?"*
- *"My grandmother broke her hip like you did, and she was never the same."*

What to Do
- Remember that in general, shorter, more frequent visits are better than longer, less frequent ones. Call before you plan to visit, and ask the caregiver, or the person who is recovering, to be honest with you about the timing and length of visits.
- Offer encouragement; *"It takes a long time to recover from an injury like you had; I can see progress, even if you cannot," "You're walking more steadily today!" "My uncle had a stroke and he continued to recover, little by little, for many months."*

- Send Mylar balloons rather than flowers to someone in the hospital; balloons require no care and are easy to move around the room or from room to room.
- Check if the hospital has a site where you can e-mail patients. It might cost money for the person to e-mail back, so just offer words of encouragement and give news, don't ask questions the person might feel obligated to answer.
- Bring photos of friends and/or family for the person to have at his bedside (in the hospital), and, if his condition is appropriate, magazines, newspapers, DVDs, etc.
- Offer to take the person for a walk, a drive, to an appointment, or even out to lunch or dinner depending on his condition.
- Call, send a card, or e-mail the person to offer support and encouragement. Include a poem, quote, or appropriate Bible Verse like Ps. 91, Matt. 11:28-30, Phill. 4:13, 1 Pet. 5:7, Heb. 13:5b-6.
- When people face a life-changing event, their faith often becomes stronger, and even if the person was not a believer, he or she might be thinking more about faith and religion. Be open to signals that the person wants to talk, and be ready to share your faith.
- Turn the conversation to subjects other than the person's illness or injury; talk about the weather, mutual friends, family, etc. (If the person wants to recount the accident or illness, that's OK; let him take the lead in where the conversation turns.)
- Offer to use your skills and talents to help during the recovery process; give the person a haircut, organize the hospital bills and records, cook meals, shop, give him a massage, etc.
- Accept his feelings and emotions of hope, discouragement, despair, and so on. There are no 'right' or 'wrong' feelings.

Don't . . .
- . . . stop calling or visiting.
- . . . offer false hope or overstate the progress that the person is making.
- . . . question medical treatment and care unless you are qualified to do so.

To the Caregiver
(Use these suggestions in addition to those earlier in the chapter.)

What to Say
- *"You are doing a great job in a stressful situation."*
- *"It's OK to be tired/frustrated/sad/angry/upset."*
- *"It's OK to need a break/cry/yell."*
- *"This must get overwhelming at times; if you ever want to talk, you can always call me."*
- *"I would like to bring you dinner this week; would tonight work, or would later in the week be better?"*
- *"On my way to visit this afternoon, I have to stop at the grocery store. What do you need?"*

What Not to Say
- *"You should just put her in a nursing home."*
- *"He'll never change. You'll have your hands full!"*
- *"It's going to be too hard for you. You can't care for her at home."*
- *"He will not recover."*

What to Do
- Pray for the caregiver's strength and peace of mind.
- Send supportive cards or e-mails to the caregiver. Include an encouraging quote, poem, or verse, perhaps Ps. 91:15, 2 Cor. 9:8, or Phillip. 4:9.
- Bring a meal—it's OK to bring a take-out meal! The caregiver still does not have to plan or prepare it.
- Offer to stay with the ill/injured person so the caregiver can take a break, or take a nap.
- The caregiver may hit a slump, similar to Post Traumatic Stress Syndrome, 6-12 months after the illness or injury. Be sensitive to signs he or she is 'slumping'—being very tired, discouraged, and/or overwhelmed. Show extra support at this time by calling, bringing meals, taking the ill or injured person to appointments, staying with the ill or injured person so the caregiver can get out

of the house, inviting the caregiver out to lunch or a movie, and so on.
- Listen to the caregiver talk; allow him or her to express feelings of frustration, anger, sadness, disappointment, and so on.

Don't . . .
- . . . question the medical treatment his/her loved one is receiving.
- . . . tell the person how he should or should not feel.

Chronic (long-term) Illness

Chronic illnesses include (but are not limited to) Multiple Sclerosis, cancer (see later in the chapter if the cancer becomes terminal), Chronic Fatigue Syndrome, Rheumatoid Arthritis, Crohn's Disease, and so on. People suffering from these diseases have remissions and exacerbations—times in which the symptoms of the illness are less and more severe.

When Someone is Diagnosed with a Chronic Illness

What to Say
- *"I'm so sorry!"*
- *"You will be in my prayers."*
- *"I don't know much about _____ (disease). Do you mind telling me a little bit about it?"*
- *"What is next treatment-wise?"*
- *"How are you doing, now that you have the doctor's report?"*
- *"It is OK to be sad/angry/discouraged/down."*
- *"It is OK to yell/cry/scream/be mad at God."*

What Not to Say
- *"Maybe the tests were wrong."*
- *"I know you'll be completely cured."*
- *"Don't be upset!"*
- *"God must be trying to get your attention."*

- *"At least you don't have _____(disease). That would be much worse!"*
- *"It's not as bad as being sick with _____(disease)".*

What to Do
- Pray for your friend's peace of mind, symptoms to be alleviated, and healing, according to God's will. Pray for your friend to accept God's will.
- Allow the person to share his or her feelings with you; accept whatever feelings she expresses.
- Offer to research the disease and treatment options if your friend wants you to.
- Offer to accompany your friend on doctor visits.
- Help your friend continue her activities and projects if she wants to; drive her to meetings, pick up supplies for her, and so on.
- Support your friend if she decides to cut out extra activities due to her illness.
- If the disease or treatment causes nausea, tiredness, weakness, or other adverse symptoms, help your friend accordingly; provide meals for her family, clean or shop for her, and so on.
- Offer the following Bible verses as support; Ps. 91, Matt. 6:25-34, Phillip. 4:13, 19, 1 Pet. 5:7, Heb. 13:5b-6.

Don't . . .
- . . . judge or criticize your friend's feelings.
- . . . ignore the fact that your friend has been diagnosed with a chronic illness; it's OK to talk about it.
- . . . send a get-well card; the person will not get well! Instead, send a thinking-of-you card.
- . . . have preconceived notions about how your friend should act or feel after being diagnosed with a chronic disease; a wide range of feelings is normal.
- . . . question the treatment unless you are a medical professional.

Ongoing—Weeks and Months after the Diagnosis

What to Say
- *"How are you doing today?"* (People with a chronic illness have remissions and exacerbations of that illness, and it is not always possible to tell how they are feeling from outward appearances alone.)
- *"What can I do to help?"* (It's OK to ask this frequently; you can't tell from outward appearances how someone is doing. From day to day your friend's need for assistance may change.)
- *"You're looking better today than you did last week."*
- *"Improvements can seem slow, but look how much better you're doing than last month!"*

What Not to Say
- *"I just know you'll be better than ever in no time."* (Don't offer false encouragement.)
- *"Don't get so upset and down."* (Don't tell someone how to feel!)
- *"Are you sure your doctor is giving you the right treatments?"*

What to Do
- Pray for the person to heal, or for his or her specific needs—to be relieved of pain, regain energy—according to God's will. Pray for your friend to accept God's will.
- If the person is confined to home, visit. Bring something to hold his interest (magazines, a book, or puzzle, depending on his interests and abilities).
- Visit. Visits can be brief; phone before you visit to determine a good time and how long a visit the person can tolerate. Don't forget to ask if you can take her something.
- Realize that she might be having pain or other symptoms without exhibiting outward signs of those symptoms.
- Offer to accompany the person on doctor visits.
- Acknowledge her limitations, but be encouraging; *"You're right, your walking is unsteady. But I know the therapists are working with you to improve your balance."*

- Be willing to talk about anything the person wants to talk about, even if it's death or dying. (See *"What to Say to Someone Who is Dying"* later in this chapter.)
- Notice and comment on improvements.
- Send cards or e-mails of support or encouragement. Include encouraging sayings, poems, or Bible Verses (2 Cor. 7:10, Ps. 30:5, Ps. 119:50).

Don't . . .
- . . . stop visiting!
- . . . send a get-well card; the person is not going to get well. Instead, send a thinking-of-you card.
- . . . assume because a person looks good she is not feeling symptoms of the disease.
- . . . question the person's doctors, medications, treatments, etc., unless you are a professional medical person.
- . . . compare the person's course of disease, treatment, or recovery, to anyone else's—everyone's case is different.

When a Child has a Chronic Illness

When a child is sick, the whole family, including the child's siblings, is affected and needs encouragement and support. Treatment and follow-up will likely involve many visits to doctors and other therapists. These visits can be exhausting both physically and mentally, to the parents as well as the ill child. The change in routine will affect the whole family.

What to Say
- *"I'm so sorry to hear she is sick! How are you doing with it all?"*
- *"I don't know much about that disease; do you mind telling me about it?"*
- *"Did you get the doctor's report? How are you doing after hearing the report?"*
- *"You are all in our thoughts and prayers. Is there something specific you'd like me to pray about?"*

- "How can I help?" "Can I pick the kids up from school today?" "I would like to bring supper over; would tomorrow be a good day to do that?"

To the child;
- "How are you today?"
- "I'm so sorry you are sick! Would you like to tell me about it?"
- "What happened at the doctor's office today?"

What Not to Say
- "She looks like she is fine; is she just faking it to get out of school?"
- "Couldn't you have prevented this?"
- "Wow, that's pretty bad, isn't it?"

To the child;
- "You don't look like you're in pain; you're getting around just fine! How can you say it hurts?"

What to Do
- Pray for the child's healing or relief from symptoms, and for God's peace and acceptance for the whole family.
- Treat even sick kids like kids—talk, read, joke with them as if they were not sick.
- Realize that the child could be in pain even if she or he does not show outward signs of pain.
- Offer to take a meal to give the parents a break from cooking.
- Offer to stay with the sick child so parents can attend events of the other children.
- Offer to take other children shopping or on an outing, drive to or from activities, or pick up groceries or prescriptions.

Don't . . .
- . . . encourage or offer to do anything to/with/for the child that the parents have not said is OK.
- . . . question the child's medical treatment.

When Someone Has a Severe/Terminal Illness

What to Say
- *"I'm so sorry."*
- *"How are you doing?"*
- *"I just don't know what to say."*
- *"What can I do for you?"*
- *If you don't want to talk about the details that's fine—I just want to know in general how you are doing."*
- *"It's OK to be angry/sad/laugh/cry."*
- *"It's OK to be mad at God!"*
- *"How are you feeling, now that you've gotten the test results back?"*
- *"Remember, this is all in God's plan."*
- *"Have faith ... sometimes that's all we can do."*
- *"God is with you every step of the way."*

What Not to Say
- *"Aren't you afraid of dying?"*
- *"Do you think you have good doctors?"*
- *"Don't worry, I just know everything will work out perfectly."*
- *"I've heard that can be really painful ... "* (It is OK to agree with the person if she tells you this about the disease, but don't bring up negative aspects of the disease or treatment.)

What to Do
- Pray for the right words to say, and for guidance as to how you can help your friend through this time.
- Share your faith; people who did not believe in God, or whose faith is weak, may be ready to turn to God during times of crisis like a severe or terminal illness.
- Enjoy the time you are able to spend with your friend, and don't feel guilty when you cannot spend time with her.
- Tell positive stories of people you've known or read about who have recovered from what your friend is suffering from.
- If your friend says the prognosis is positive, believe her, and rejoice with her.

- If your friend gets a negative report, believe her, and comfort her.
- Know it's OK to be funny—people still have a sense of humor, even when they're sick. It's usually OK to make jokes and laugh; take your cue from the person who is ill.
- Give your ill friend the phone number of people who have survived the illness she is suffering from.
- Realize that it's OK to admit that you are afraid or don't know what to say.
- Allow your friend to share her true feelings with you, without judging her on how she 'should' or 'should not' feel. Let her express her true feelings; allow her to cry, yell, be mad at God, and so on.
- Actively listen to see how you can help your friend. Some people want company when they're sick, others do not. Some people want to talk about the details of their illness and treatments, while others do not. Follow your friend's lead.
- Reassure your friend that it is OK to rest, sleep, and skip activities and events.
- Encourage and assist your friend if she wants to continue her activities, or start new projects.
- Offer to help using your talents and strengths; if you are comfortable in a medical environment, offer to accompany your friend to doctor visits or keep her company while she's in the hospital. If you can cut hair, give massages, arrange flowers, read expressively, sing, or apply make-up, use those skills to give your friend a lift. If you are good at organizing, arrange (with your friend's approval) people to transport her kids to school, take meals to the family, purchase groceries and clean the house.
- Offer to help connect your friend with services like Home Health, Meals on Wheels, Hospice, etc.
- Send cards or e-mails with comforting and encouraging poems and Bible verses; Ps. 23, Ps. 91, Matt. 6:25-34, 2 Cor. 5:1-7, Phillip. 4:13, 1 Pet. 5:7, Heb. 13:5b-6.

Don't . . .
- . . . avoid your friend, or stop calling her due to your discomfort about her illness.
- . . . put pressure on your friend to 'be brave' . . . let her be open with her true feelings when the two of you are together.
- . . . dwell on bad news; listen if she wants to talk about it, but follow her lead if she wants to talk about something else.
- . . . compare her to someone else who kept up with all of activities, or painted, or wrote a book, or took on a project, while sick, undergoing radiation or chemotherapy, or recovering from surgery.
- . . . judge her by what she does or doesn't do or how she acts.
- . . . discourage your friend from being as active as she wants to be, as long as it is OK with her doctor.

Babies and Children with Special Needs and/or a Disability

When a Baby is Born with Special Needs or a Disability

Everyone dreams of the perfect baby, and parents and family members can be devastated if a baby is born with special needs or a disability, whether it is easily corrected or will cause life-long problems.

What to Say
- *"You and the baby and your family are in my prayers! What would you like me to pray for?"*
- *"God is watching over all of you; He loves your baby very, very much!"*
- *"I'm so sorry!"*
- *"It will be hard, but you are strong. When you don't feel strong, I will be there to help and listen, and there are many other people who love you and will help too."*
- *"I don't know much about that disease/problems — do you mind telling me about it?"*
- *"It must be hard for you to see the baby struggling/in pain."*

- *"It must be very frustrating and sad sometimes."*
- If the illness/disability is temporary (will be repaired by surgery or heal with time), *"I know this is very hard right now, but in six months, if it's God's will, she will be much better! We will be here to help you through this rough time."*

What Not to Say
- *"Is it something you could have prevented?"*
- *"Life is going to be really hard for him!"* (The parents already know this!)
- *"Think of all the children who have a more severe form of his disability, or cancer, and are worse off than he is."* (The situation is bad enough for the parents; it doesn't help to compare.)
- *"Your situation is not as bad as . . ."*

What to Do
- Pray for the parents to have peace, and for God to guide them in their decision-making. Pray for the doctors and all who care for the baby.
- Carefully observe the parents' reactions to your questions and respond accordingly; some parents might find it therapeutic to talk about what is happening, while others might not want to talk extensively about it.
- Allow the parents to share their fear and anxiety with you. Listen and accept their thoughts and feelings.
- Voice your support of medical decisions the parents must make. (If you do not agree with their decisions, keep it to yourself or talk about it to a counselor or clergy person, not with the parents.)
- When you see the baby, or photos of him, say something positive about his silky hair, beautiful eyes, long fingers, etc.
- Call the baby by name; touch his head, stroke his arm.
- Ask what you can do to help with the other children.
- Offer to sit with the baby, either at home or in the hospital, so the parents can get some sleep, do errands, or spend time with their other children.

- Remember the grandparents and other extended family members, who are suffering, too.
- Send a thinking-of-you card with an appropriate poem or verse; Ps. 23, Ps. 91, Matt. 19:14-15, Phillip. 4:13, 19, 1 Pet. 5:7, Heb. 13:5b-6.

Don't ...
- ... refer to the baby as "it."
- ... tell scary stories about the disease or sick children.
- ... voice disagreement with or disapproval of medical decisions the parents make.
- ... question the child's doctors or treatment the child is getting.
- ... minimize the child's disability by comparing it to children who might be 'worse off,' or sicker than their child. This does not ease their worry or sadness about their own child.

If Your Baby Has Special Needs

What to Say
- *"Thank you for caring!"*
- *"Please pray for ... "*
- *"Could you please help by ... taking the other kids to school/ going with the baby and I to the doctor/staying at the hospital with the baby so I can go home and get some sleep/feed the dog."*

What Not to Say
- *"Quit asking me stupid questions!"* (Even if you are tired of questions, try to say that in a polite way.)

What to Do
- Point out your baby's pretty eyes, delicate toes.
- Accept help when it is offered.
- Tell people what you'd like them to pray for.
- If you're comfortable doing so, educate people about your child's challenges.

Don't . . .
- . . . turn down help you need.

An Older Child With a Disability

What to Say

To the parent or the child;
- *"Can I open the door for you/help you reach that?"*
- *"It must be frustrating, sometimes, to be different/to have a child with such challenges."*
- *"I admire you for the way you are coping with your challenges; you're always so cheerful!"*
- *"How is* (name of child) *doing?"*

To the parent;
- *"How are you doing?"*
- *"You're doing a great job arranging doctor's appointments and taking care of your son!"*
- *"What can I do to help?"*
- *"Do you mind if I ask you about your child's disability?"*

What Not to Say
- To the parent; *"I just know you're going to go to heaven because of all you've done to take care of your child!"* (Parents don't take care of their child to get to heaven, and this belief is not in agreement with all religions.)
- *"I know you're strong because God would never give you more than you can bear."* (This may be taken as a criticism if the parent or disabled person does not feel strong; at times the parents may feel as if they cannot bear their child being disabled!)
- *"Think of all the children who have cancer or are worse off than he is."*
- *"What's wrong with him?"*

What to Do
- Use seeing a disabled child or person as an opportunity to teach your child about accepting everyone.
- Talk naturally and respectfully to the person who is disabled.
- If the person is in a wheelchair, kneel or sit, so you're at eye level, when talking to him.
- Accept the child's and/or parent's feelings of anger, sadness, anxiety, and worry. Allow them to talk with you about those feelings.

Don't . . .
- . . . touch a disabled child without getting permission from his or her parents.
- . . . take pictures or videos without permission from the child or his parents.
- . . . try to minimize the anxiety, sadness, and worry, that the parents are feeling. They may be feeling these emotions even if their child is stable or improving at the time.
- . . . offer a disabled child money, toys, or treats, that you would not offer a non-disabled child. It's insulting to treat a disabled child differently than you would other children, or with pity.
- . . . stare at the child.
- . . . make assumptions about the person's mental or physical abilities.
- . . . make fun of a disabled child, or allow your children to.

Chapter 7

Various Tricky, Sticky, Uncomfortable Situations

This chapter touches on a wide variety of tricky, sticky, uncomfortable situations, at least some of which you're likely to face. These situations are uncomfortable, even when you do have the right words to say. Many situations presented here do not require an immediate response, but after a time, you might feel as if you need to intervene in some way.

In many of these scenarios you'll be telling the person involved something he or she probably won't like hearing. Before you intervene, examine your motives. Why do you want to share your thoughts and opinions with the person? If your actions are not motivated by the desire to truly help the person having a problem, you probably should not do or say anything. No matter uncomfortable it may be, if your motives are pure, you are doing the right thing by speaking up.

General Guidelines for Telling Someone Something They Don't want to Hear

What to Say
- *"It is hard for me to say this . . . "*
- *"You probably don't want to hear this, but it's very important . . . "*
- *"I'm very concerned about . . . "*
- *"It would be easier for me to let this issue go, but it involves your safety and the safety of others . . . "*
- *"I feel very strongly about this and so want to tell you what I think . . . "*
- *"This is probably hard for you to hear, but I've had training in this area, and you need to seek help."*
- *"I love you very much, and don't want to hurt you by saying this . . . "*

What Not to Say
- *"You can really be a jerk, and here's one example . . . "*
- *"You absolutely have to stop doing this stupid thing you so stubbornly have been doing . . . "*
- *"You never help out and always take advantage of others."*

What to Do
- Pray for guidance as to if you should approach the person, and if so, the words to say.
- Before you confront the person, consider the long-term issues of doing so. Confronting someone can lead to a stress in friendship, or may even cause the person to break off the friendship completely.
- Plan for the conversation ahead of time; where and when it will take place, the points you want to make, etc.
- Consider having someone with you if you anticipate a difficult scene or want someone to witness what happens (if the person you're confronting has a history of lying, for example).
- Say a brief prayer, asking for the right words, and take a deep breath before you start to speak.

- Speak calmly yet firmly.
- When you talk, focus on the message you want to get across, not your emotions.
- Respond to the person calmly, and with facts.
- Be prepared for any reaction from the person you're talking with; he or she may be angry, or grateful to you for bringing up the issue.

Don't . . .
- . . . be overly emotional during the conversation.
- . . . confront/approach the person if he or she is inebriated or very angry.
- . . . say anything unkind, or act in a mean or cruel manner.
- . . . make a big scene in public.

Two Friends have a Falling Out

What to Say
- "I plan to remain friends with both of you."
- "I'm not going to repeat what _____ (other friend) and I talk about; I don't intend to talk about either of you to the other."

What Not to Say
- "I don't think I'll repeat anything you say, to her . . . it depends what it is."

What to Do
- Pray about your involvement and any attempt to help resolve the conflict.
- Be matter-of-fact if one friend asks about your plans and you're spending time with the other friend.
- Ask each friend if they'd like to talk about the problem with you or someone as a mediator.

Don't . . .
- . . . criticize or talk about the friend you're not with.
- . . . push too hard for the friends to make up.
- . . . attempt to get the friends together without telling them what you're doing.

Someone Asks You for a Job Reference

What if a friend asks you to recommend him for a job in your company, or write a reference for him? Of course, if he is qualified you'll probably be happy to do it. If, however, the person is not qualified, you would be lying if you wrote a positive reference or recommended the person for the job. You won't gain points with your employer if someone who is not qualified joins the company on your recommendation, and you are not doing your friend a favor if he takes a job he isn't qualified for.

What to Say
- *"I'm not sure the job would be right for you . . . "*
- *"I haven't seen or talked to you for awhile! Let's get together and catch up with what you've been doing professionally."* (The person might realize he was imposing by asking you for a recommendation, or you might meet and find that he has changed and is qualified for the job.)
- *"I'm sorry, I don't feel comfortable doing that for a friend, in case it doesn't work out."*
- *"I don't think I'd be the best person to do this for you, since I have not worked with you in that capacity."*
- If the person is qualified, you can say, *"I'll recommend you, but there are other applicants, so I cannot guarantee you'll get the job."*

What Not to Say
- *"I'm positive I can get you the job!"*
- *"I'll give you a great reference!"* (if that is not true).

What to Do
- Consider giving a carefully worded reference, so the person hiring can read between the lines; *"Carmen gets small projects done on time and remembers all of her co-workers birthdays."*
- Be honest with the person as to why you are not comfortable recommending him for the job.

Don't . . .
- . . . write a recommendation or give a reference if you can't do so honestly.

A Friend is in an Abusive Relationship

Although 85% of domestic abuse is by a man, upon a woman, a small percentage of men are abused by women they are married to or in a relationship with. One of four people will experience domestic violence during his or her life. Here's how you can help if you suspect or know of abuse.

What to Say
- *"You're in my thoughts and prayers!"*
- *"I'm here for me if you need me, any time of the day or night."*
- *"Think about what would be best for your children and for you."*
- *"I am afraid for your safety."*
- *"You deserve better than to be hurt."*
- *"Here is the phone number and address of a woman's shelter."*
- *"I know a counselor who works with battered women; would you like me to make an appointment for you and take you to it?"*

What Not to Say
- *"You need to just leave!"* (Your friend needs to make that decision on her own.)
- *"Everything will be just fine, don't you worry."*
- *"Here's what you have to do . . . "*

What to Do
- Educate yourself on the issue of abuse; just type "domestic abuse" into your search engine, ask the librarian where the books about domestic abuse are located in the library, or call a woman's shelter in your area.
- Educate yourself about nearby shelters, legal aid, and other resources.
- Follow the recommendations of a local women's shelter as to how you can best help your friend.
- Reassure the victim that the abuse is not his or her fault.
- Build your friend's self-esteem by pointing out her strengths and skills.
- Call the police if you witness abuse.
- Assure your friend that you are willing to listen.
- Tell the person you are concerned for her safety and well-being.
- Reassure her of your love and support, and the availability of organizations that will help women in her situation.
- Be non-judgmental of her decisions, even if they're not the decisions you would make.
- Pray for your friend to have the strength to make the right decision.
- Be a calm and stable presence in your friend's life.
- Let her call a lawyer, an abuse hotline, her parents, etc., from your home; give her privacy while she does so.
- Be very careful when making decisions to as how to help your friend by taking her into your home, picking her up from her home, giving her money, and so on. You could be putting yourself, your family, and your friend and her family in danger if you go about it the wrong way and her husband or boyfriend is violent.
- Be patient with your friend as she works through her situation.
- Remember that you cannot force the person to leave the relationship; she has to make that decision on her own.

Don't . . .
- . . . criticize your friend for her decisions, even if she leaves and then returns to the abusive person. She needs your support even more at this time.
- . . . put yourself or your family in danger.

If a Friend Has been Sexually Assaulted

Someone who has been sexually assaulted may seek and need help immediately after the assault, or days, weeks, or even months later.

What to Say
- *"I believe you!"*
- *"It was not your fault!"*

What Not to Say
- *"Are you sure it really happened like that?"*
- *"Did you do something to cause it?"*
- *"Are you sure he meant it that way?"*

What to Do
- Allow your friend to stay with you; she needs to feel safe.
- Encourage your friend to seek medical attention, and take her to the hospital.
- Encourage your friend to report the assault, even if it's been some time since it occurred.
- Encourage her to seek counseling, whether you find out about the assault immediately after it happened or long after.
- Educate yourself about sexual assault via research on the internet, at your local library, or by calling a rape hotline.
- Listen to your friend talk, cry, scream; accept her emotions.

Don't . . .
- . . . force your friend to go to the hospital or call the police; strongly encourage her to do so as soon as possible, but do not

physically force her to do so. Be patient and let her be in control of when to do it.
- ... doubt what your friend says.
- ... imply that the assault was her fault, or that she could have prevented it.
- ... tell anyone that it happened, without her consent.

When a Friend is Depressed

20% of women will become depressed at some time during their lives, as will 10% of men, so chances are great that at some time you will know someone who is depressed. Signs that someone is depressed include; lack of energy; unintended weight gain or loss because of a change in eating habits; change in sleep patterns (sleeping very little or very much, or being awake during the night and sleeping all day); complains of feeling sad, 'down', depressed, 'empty' for more than two weeks, and a lack of interest in usual activities.

A person usually becomes depressed because of something that is happening in his or her life; death of a loved one, marriage problems or divorce, loss of job, illness, money problems, and so on. However, people can become depressed for no apparent reason. Here are some things you can say and do to help someone who is suffering from depression. (If you sense someone is very depressed, to the point of being suicidal, see the section on suicide in Chapter 5 of this book.)

What to Say
- *"How are you doing today?"*
- *You've seemed kind of down; do you want to talk about it?"* (Suggest counseling, discussed below, if you feel it's needed.)
- *"I had a bout of depression several years ago so I can relate to how you are feeling."*
- *"I did not want to take medication for my depression, but finally did, and it really helped me to cope with what was going on."*
- *"It is not a weakness to seek professional help."*

- *"I will call you tomorrow to see how you're doing."*
- *"I'll pick you up later so we can go out for lunch."*
- *"I'm worried because you've been so down; I think it is time for you to talk with someone who can help you better than I can, like a counselor or your pastor. Would you like me to make an appointment? I'll take you, or go with you, if you want me to."*

What Not to Say
- *"Snap out of it!"*
- *"It can't be that bad. Get over it."*
- *"You're pathetic. Quit acting that way."*

What to Do
- Pray for your friend's depression to be lifted, and if that is not God's will, for her to seek and accept the help she needs.
- Educate yourself on the subject of depression.
- Know when your friend needs more help than you can give her.
- Gently bring up the subject of her getting professional help, on an ongoing basis; sometimes it takes encouragement over time for someone to finally get the help she needs.
- If necessary, make the appointment with a psychiatrist, counselor, pastor or priest, and/or go with her or take her to the appointment.
- Encourage your friend to follow the recommendations of her counselor; if she begins taking medications, remind her that they can take up to 4-6 weeks to take effect. Encourage her to talk to her doctor if the side effects are making her reluctant to take the medication, or it does not seem to be helping her mood after 4-6 weeks.
- Send encouraging cards or e-mails; consider including Bible verses like Ps. 18:2, 28; Ps. 46:1; Ps. 55:22.
- Offer to care for her children while she goes to counseling appointments, or just so she has some time to herself.
- Accept her feelings.

Don't . . .
- . . . give up on your friend.
- . . . disregard the danger signs of suicide (see Chapter 5).
- . . . stop encouraging her to seek the help she needs.

If You Suspect a Friend is Addicted

What to Say
- *"I'll spend time with you when you're sober, but not if you've been drinking or taking drugs."*
- *"I'm very concerned about how much you are gambling/ drinking/taking drugs. I see the harm it's doing to you."*
- *"I am afraid that you might have a problem with sex/gambling/ shopping."*
- *"You are abusing drugs and hurting yourself."*
- *"You need to talk to a professional about this."*
- *"Your behaviors and actions are affecting your children."*
- *"Your friendships are suffering because of your behaviors."*

What Not to Say
- *"Just stop it!"*

What to Do
- Educate yourself via the internet or your library, on the subject of addictions, signs and symptoms, and actions you can take to help your friend.
- Pray for your friend to get the help she needs, and for God to guide you as to what to say and do.
- Set boundaries; *"Do not call me or come over if you've been drinking or using drugs."*
- Research the subject of addictions so you know how to help her, and where to refer your friend when she is ready to seek help.
- Support, encourage, and help your friend get the help she needs.
- Realize you cannot make your friend to change; be patient and continue to urge her to get help.

Don't . . .
- . . . try to talk with your friend about her addiction when she is drunk or on drugs.
- . . . cover for your friend or try to protect her from the consequences of her actions.
- . . . become enmeshed with your friend's problem to the extent that your own obligations to your family and job and home are not being met.
- . . . give money to, or otherwise enable your friend to get drugs or alcohol, or participate in gambling or her problem behavior.

After a Friend or Acquaintance has Attempted Suicide

Whether or not you knew the person was depressed or going through a hard time, it's probably a shock that someone you knew attempted suicide. However, it's important to overcome your own discomfort and shock and show support to that person after a suicide attempt, whether you say these things when the person is in the hospital or has returned home or to school or work.

What to Say
- *"You'll be OK; I'll help you get through this."*
- *"I have faith in you, that you can overcome this."*
- *"I'm so glad you did not succeed and are still here!"*
- *"God loves you not matter what."*
- *"You are important to me and to many other people."*

What Not to Say
- *"I don't want to hear about it."*
- *"I can't believe you did that!"*
- *"You couldn't even get it right when you tried to kill yourself."*
- *"You were crazy to try to do that."*

What to Do
- Welcome the person back to school, work, church, etc. It might be awkward at first, for both of you! Tell him you're glad to see him, listen if he wants to talk, and don't push if he does not want to talk about the suicide attempt.
- Include your acquaintance in conversations.
- Ask your acquaintance to sit with you at break, lunch, church or school.
- Encourage the person to see his counselor and take medications as ordered.
- Overcome your discomfort with the situation and allow the person to talk about it if he or she wants to.

Don't . . .
- . . . shut the person out at work, school, home, or church.
- . . . let your discomfort with the situation keep you from helping your friend by listening when he wants to talk about it.

Unexpected Pregnancy

When a Friend's Unmarried Child is Pregnant
A parent who is faced with a unmarried child's pregnancy is confronted with many issues and choices, and will be feeling a wide range of emotions. The following comments and suggestions are appropriate for both the child and his or her parents.

What to Say
- *"We are keeping you and your family in our prayers."*
- *"God bless you for choosing life for your baby."*
- *"I'm a good listener if you ever want to talk!"*
- *"Your child is blessed to have your love."*
- *"We will support you all whether you decide to keep the baby or put her up for adoption."*

To the parents:
- *"You taught your kids well; as parents we just can't have total control over everything they do. It is not your fault this happened! You are a good parent."*

What Not to Say

To the parents:
- *"Who is the father of the baby?"*
- *"How could she live with herself if she gave the baby up for adoption?"*
- *"How were they so dumb to get into this mess—don't they know about birth control?"*
- *"Didn't you see this coming?"*
- *"They just have to keep the baby/give the baby up for adoption."*

To the child:
- *"How could you be so dumb?"*
- *"How could you do this to your family?"*
- *"You have ruined your life!"*
- *"You have to . . ."* *"You cannot . . ."*

What to Do
- Think before you speak when you learn about the pregnancy, especially if you are shocked.
- Discourage abortion if they are considering it as an option; offer other options, provide the phone number for an adoption agency.
- Encourage the family to work with someone trained in dealing with this situation.
- Use the situation as an opportunity to talk with your kids about consequences of their choices.
- Be friendly and say *"Hello!"* when you see the child or family in church, at school, at work, or in the store.

Don't...
- ...pass on any information if you're not sure the family wants it made public.
- ...speculate as to circumstances of the pregnancy, who the father might be, if the child will be placed for adoption, and so on.
- ...plan a baby shower or give gifts unless/until you know their plans regarding adoption.
- ...lecture; express your feelings and beliefs in a way that is godly and non-critical.
- ...feel obligated to attend a baby shower or give gifts if doing so is not in accordance with your beliefs and feelings about the situation.
- ...accept plans for an abortion without expressing your pro-life beliefs. If you are reluctant to do this, remember that the life of a baby is at stake.
- ...react with shock regarding the details of paternity, plans for the baby, and so on.

If a Friend is Unexpectedly Pregnant
It might take your friend some time to get used to an unexpected pregnancy! She will appreciate your friendship and support.

What to Say
- *"How do you feel about the news?"* and then, *"Congratulations!"* or *"Oh, my!"* depending on how your friend reacts to the news that she is pregnant.
- *"It is OK to have mixed feelings about your pregnancy!"*
- *"The baby is blessed to be coming into your family."*

What Not to Say
- *"Better you than me!"*
- *"What were you thinking?"*
- *"Don't you know what causes babies?"*
- *"Do you know what can go wrong in a woman your age?"*

What to Do
- Accept your friend's feelings of confusion, joy, anger, and/or ambivalence.
- Let your friend talk, cry, yell. Accept her feelings and emotions.
- When you sense the time is right, remind her that God has His plan, and babies are a miracle and blessing.
- Discourage abortion; encourage adoption if the situation is such that the person feels she cannot give the baby a good home.

Don't . . .
- . . . buy gifts or offer to loan maternity clothes or baby supplies until your friend is ready.
- . . . criticize your friend's feelings of confusion, ambivalence, anger, or disappointment.
- . . . share the news with anyone until she says it's OK to do so.
- . . . accept plans for an abortion without expressing your pro-life views; the life of a baby is at stake!

Secrets

Revealing a Secret From Your Past

Many people have experienced events or worked through issues from their past (recent or very far back) that are not common knowledge. In your life, this could include a difficult childhood, marital problems, being the victim of domestic abuse, sexual orientation or practices, suffering from depression, having had an abortion, having given a baby up for adoption, or overcoming drug or alcohol abuse or a gambling addiction.

You might consider revealing something from your past for one of several reasons. Are you contemplating revealing a secret to ease your conscience? If so, is it worth possibly hurting the person you're telling, or others close to you? Are you telling the secret to hurt another person? Revealing it for that reason could backfire.

If you want to reveal something to 'get it off your chest', carefully consider who you tell; if you feel you need to tell someone, but don't know if or how you should, talk with your clergy person, counselor, or someone else who is removed from the situation, for objective advice on if and how to proceed.

Sometimes revealing something about your past can help another person make a difficult decision or avoid problems you had in the past. Revealing your own struggle with depression might encourage someone who is depressed to open up to you, knowing you will accept her illness, for example. Sharing your experience with an unexpected pregnancy will help someone consider the ramifications of decisions she makes about *her* unexpected pregnancy.

Here are some suggestions for sharing something from your past.

What to Say
- *"Not many people know that my husband and I struggled with infertility, so I know at least a bit of what you are going through."*
- *"I didn't tell many people at the time, but several years ago I struggled with depression. I felt like no one else understood. I want to tell you that I understand, and hope I can help you through this."*
- *"My husband and I had marital problems long ago, but I still remember how I felt. I'm here to talk if you ever want to. Whatever we talk about will be just between us."*
- *"I'd like to tell you about something that happened in my life and how I dealt with it. Perhaps it will help you make your decision."*
- *"My parents hit me when I was a kid and I didn't know who to turn to. I'd like to help you as you are dealing with your abuse."*

What Not to Say
- *"I did the right thing, and if you're ever in the situation you should do the same thing."*

What to Do
- Carefully consider the ramifications of sharing your experience; secrets cannot be un-told.
- When you tell someone a secret, do so in privacy, and when you have plenty of time to discuss it.
- Give the person you told space and time to think about what you've said, after you've told your secret, especially if it's disturbing or surprising information.

Don't . . .
- . . . share a secret unless you are sure you're doing so with the right motives.
- . . . tell the secret to anyone unless you are sure that the person you are telling will not share the information, or unless you would be comfortable if he or she does share the information with other people.
- . . . expect the person to take the same steps you did when you were in the situation.

When a Friend Shares a Secret

What to Say
- "I'm so glad you told me that you've been through what I'm facing. I've felt so alone!"
- "I had no idea you were married before. Our friendship will not change because of it."
- "I did not know you gave a baby up for adoption, but you did the right thing! Thank you for trusting me enough to tell me."
- "That's a big secret you've been carrying! I'm glad you told me. I can tell it's something you regret, and I know God will forgive you if you ask Him."
- "Do you mind if I ask you a few questions about what you just told me?"
- "That happened a long time ago, and you've certainly made amends for it."
- "Would you like me to pray with you or for you?"

A friend might share her secret drug or gambling addiction, child abuse, or thoughts of suicide, as a cry for help. If a friend shares a secret that is potentially harmful to her or someone else, you must tell the proper authorities, or people involved—Child Protective Services, a clergy person, the police, or spouse. Say to the person;
- *"You can't handle this alone, and neither can I. We need to tell someone who can help."*
- *"I am so sorry you're going through this! I know there is help out there, and I will be with you every step of the day."*

If a friend reveals a secret that is in contrast with your morals—she is having an affair, for example, or stealing from her place of employment—calmly tell her your feelings and what you intend to do or not do. Depending on the situation, you might feel obligated to report the person to the proper authorities.
- *"You're having an affair? That is not the way to solve a marriage problem."*
- *"Stealing from work is a crime; you must stop. I will help you find a counselor, or go with you to talk to your boss."*
- *"I will not be a part of helping you cover that up, but I will help you resolve it."*
- *"What you are doing is not in agreement with God's teachings. He will forgive you, if you stop what you are doing and ask for forgiveness. I would like to help you get right with Him."*

What Not to Say
- *"Oh my gosh! I can't believe you were that dumb!"*
- *"I had that exact same experience!"* (saying this diminishes the person's experience).
- *"Here's what you need to do . . . "*
- *"You really did that?"*

What to Do
- Take a deep breath before you say anything!
- If your friend is considering suicide, see that section in Chapter 5.

- Try to discern why your friend is telling you the secret, and respond accordingly. If she feels guilty for something she's done in the past, and has remedied the situation or is sincerely regretful, reassure her that she did what she thought was best at the time.
- Share Bible verses appropriate to her situation.
- Remind her of God's forgiveness.
- Listen to your friend's secret; accept her emotions related to it.
- Reassure your friend that her secret does not change your friendship.

Don't ...
- ... act so shocked that she becomes uncomfortable that she told you the secret.
- ... speak before thinking.
- ... agree with what the person has done, or is planning, if it is contrary to your beliefs or morals.

Invitations and Get-togethers

When Someone Asks for an Invitation

You're planning your wedding, a dinner party, or the birth of your baby, and have chosen the guests (or people you want to attend the birth) carefully. But you see someone (someone you do not intend to invite) on the street and they ask, *"Where is my invitation? Do you need my address?" "Can I be in the delivery room when you have the baby?"*

Here are some suggestions for getting out of that sticky situation.

What to Say
- *"I'm so sorry, but we had to keep the guest list small."*
- *"We haven't been in touch for years! I didn't even know if you were still in town. Let's plan to get together after the wedding and catch up!"*

- *"My fiance' and I both have huge families, so we really had to limit the other friends we invited. Let's go out for lunch next month and I'll show you the pictures from the wedding."*
- *"We wish we could invite every single special person in our lives, but had to limit the number."*
- *"We're only inviting family this time."*
- *"You wouldn't know anyone at this party and we didn't want you to be uncomfortable. We're having another celebration soon, with the group of people you know well."*
- *"The hospital limits the number of people who can be present at the birth. We'll call you as soon as we're home, and you can come and visit the new baby."*
- *"Childbirth is an extremely private event to me! I'll let you know when we're ready for visitors after the baby is born."*

What Not to Say
- *"Um, er, well . . . we kind of couldn't invite everyone . . ."*
- *"Are you kidding? There's no way you'd fit in with this group."*
- *"I will mail it tomorrow."* (Don't say this if you're hoping the person will forget he asked for the invitation; you'll just cringe every time the phone rings! It's better to tell the truth right away.)

What to Do
- Be kind as you turn down the person's request, and then change the subject so as not to make the person who asked uncomfortable (although it's hard to embarrass someone so forward as to ask for an invitation).

Don't . . .
- . . . invite someone because she asked and you feel guilty for not doing so.

If Someone Wants to Invite Another Guest to Attend with Him
What do you do when you've carefully planned a get-together, and someone calls at the last minute to see if she can bring a visiting friend or family member?

What to Say
- *"I really don't have room to squeeze any more people in—sorry!"*
- *"The menu includes individual fish/quail that I had to specially order, and I just don't have enough. I hope you'll be able to join us at the next party."*
- If you don't mind if another person attends, but are worried about having enough food, say, *"We would love to have your sister as another guest! Would you mind bringing bread/salad/chips/dessert?"*

What Not to Say
- *"How rude to even ask!"*

What to Do
- Think before you answer; if the guest will have to spend a holiday or evening alone, or you'll miss the company of the person you originally invited (if you don't invite the guest), having an extra person would probably be worth the minor inconvenience. You might even make a new friend.

Don't ...
- ... feel obligated to include someone who you truly don't want at the gathering—someone who has a reputation of becoming drunk and obnoxious or starting fights, for example.
- ... lose sight of the objective of having a party or get-together—presumably to have fun with friends.

Asking Awkward Questions

Sometimes it's necessary to ask questions to get information you need. This can be uncomfortable if you're afraid the person you're asking will think you don't trust him or are overly cautious. However, questions (even awkward ones) are sometimes necessary to assure your kids' safety, or your own. Being open about your feelings will diffuse some of the awkwardness.

What to Say
- *"This is an awkward question for me to ask, but I really need to know . . . "*
- *"I know this is kind of an intrusive question, but the safety of my kids is my priority, so I need to know, do you have guns in your home?"*
- *"My husband and I agreed that before our kids ride with anyone, we would always ask if they use seatbelts all the time. If this isn't convenient for you, we will take our kids and yours to the party."*
- *"I don't mean to be rude by asking this; what will you be serving for supper? I have to ask because I'm very allergic to nuts; I can't even be in the same room as peanuts. I don't want you to go to any extra trouble, so will turn down your kind invitation if you were planning to serve something with nuts in it."*
- *"Who will be driving the kids? I'm asking because I'm not comfortable with teens driving other teens. If there are not enough adult drivers available, I will drive my child and can take several more children."*
- After you receive the answer; *"Thank you for your honesty."*

What Not to Say
- *"I can't believe that's your answer!"*

What to Do
- Ask in a pleasant voice.
- Ask the question in private, and well ahead of the event in case the answer makes different arrangements necessary.
- Accept the answer even if it's not what you wanted to hear.
- Be prepared for the person to be defensive about the question, and explain why you're asking.

Don't . . .
- . . . let your discomfort keep you from assuring your safety or that of your children or family.
- . . . act shocked at the answer.

Foot-in-Mouth Disease—When You Accidentally put Your Foot in Your Mouth

Sticky moments come in all shapes and sizes! Here is an example that happened to me when I ran into an old friend in the store.

Friend: *"Well, do I look old enough to be a grandfather?"*
Me: *"No! Congratulations!"*
Friend: *"Well, my daughter is pregnant and only 16 years old. She should graduate soon."*
Me: *"Oh. I'm sorry. Do you like the father of the baby?"*
Friend: *"He's not in the picture."*
Me: *"Well . . . at least she's still in school."*
Friend: (pause) *"Actually she dropped out and is working on her GED."*
Me: (searching for something encouraging to say) *"Um . . . Well I'm sure she's not on drugs or anything like that."*
Friend: (longer pause) *"Not now she's not, but she did experiment with them last year . . ."*
Me: (desperately trying to find a positive side to the situation) *"Well, if she was still on drugs she'd probably be in jail; at least she's not there!"*
Friend: *"She was recently arrested for shoplifting and was almost thrown in jail . . ."*
Me: (finally giving up trying to find something positive in this situation) *"She and your family will be in my prayers."*

So you see, sometimes in an attempt to find something positive in a situation, you just make it more uncomfortable. Now of course if this hadn't been a good, long-time friend, I would not have attempted to find something positive in these circumstances. He understood, and was not upset by my gaffes.

We've all been witness to—or maybe even created—foot-in-mouth moments. Here's how to extricate yourself as graciously as possible.

What to Say
- You congratulate someone on her pregnancy . . . and then find the added pounds are from bagels, not baby. *"Oh, my, I couldn't*

- *be more embarrassed! I'm so sorry!"* Then, drop the subject. Going on about it will just embarrass the person more.
- You're with a carload of people, and harshly criticize divorce, commenting that most people are just too lazy to work to remain married. Then you find out the driver has been divorced several times. *"I am so sorry I said that. Obviously, I don't know your circumstances, and should not judge."*
- You tell an ethnic joke, then someone who heard it mentions that he is a part of the group you just put down. *"I'm so sorry. I did not mean to offend you or anyone else. Please forgive me. I will not tell that joke again!"*
- You criticize the way a program at school or church was put together, then find out the person you're talking to was the one to organize the event. *"Gosh, I did not realize you arranged all of this! I know how much work it is, and I'm sorry I was critical."*
- *"I'm so very, very sorry I said that!"*
- *"I'm so embarrassed that I said that! I was just trying to break the ice and happened to see your wife and made that dumb comment."*

What Not to Say
- *"I didn't mean she looked 'witchy,' I meant 'witty!' "* (A feeble attempt will be seen as such and just cause more embarrassment.)
- *"Oh, don't be so sensitive! Everybody tells those jokes."*

What to Do
- Obviously, it's always better to think first and speak later! If you have any doubt at all if what you are about to say is appropriate, don't say it.
- Apologize sincerely, and then drop the subject. Apologizing over and over or becoming extremely emotional will embarrass everyone more. If you feel it is necessary, follow up with a brief note or e-mail of apology the next day.
- It is always best to apologize in person, but it is OK to do so via e-mail if you don't realize until later what you said might have been inappropriate.

Don't . . .
- . . . try too hard to make the situation better by over-apologizing.
- . . . burst into tears or become overly emotional about your misspeak; it will only make the matter more obvious and embarrassing to everyone.

Is it Good News Or Bad News?

When You Don't Know if Someone's News is Good or Bad
Don't assume that news that seems to be 'good' or 'bad' really is; some blessings are hidden or mixed. The 'bad' news that someone is moving away from a long-time home could also be 'good' news if it involves a fantastic job opportunity. A husband leaving the family seems to be 'bad' news if his long-term abuse is not known. A son going to jail seems like a negative event unless you know it is just what the parents prayed for, to force the child to face his problems. A wedding appears to be a happy event, unless the marriage is entered into under less-than-ideal circumstances.

Be sensitive to the verbal and non-verbal signals, as well as the actual words, of the person who announces the news; if she tells you in a happy, excited voice, it's probably good news; if her voice is sad, or subdued, it might actually be bad news. A huge smile usually indicates good news, while a neutral expression or frown signals not-so-good news. A person might be reluctant to share feelings that are mixed or contrary to what he thinks he 'should' be feeling; ask a few questions and you'll offer your friend a chance to share what is really happening.

What to Say
If you're not sure if the news is good or bad, open up the channels of communication by saying one of the following:
- *"Is that good news or bad?"*
- *"Wow—tell me more . . . "* (This non-judgmental response gives the person an opening to tell you what is really happening.)
- *"And how do you feel about that?"*

- If a marriage is announced, say, *"How long have they known each other?"* and take your cue from the verbal and non-verbal signals of the answer.
- If someone is moving, ask, *"What takes you so far away? How do you feel about moving there?"*
- If a family member or spouse moved out of the person's home, ask, *"How are things going without him around?"* (This question allows the person to say what he truly feels.)

What Not to Say
- *"Oh my gosh, that's absolutely the most horrible thing I can imagine happening!"* or, *"That's got to be the most wonderful news I've ever heard!"* It's hard to change your view after making such a strong statement.

What to Do
- Observe the person's facial expression and tone of voice before responding to the news.
- If you reacted inappropriately say, *"Well, then I guess that is good news!"* or, *"I'm sorry it's not a happy situation after all."*

Don't . . .
- . . . hesitate to come right out and ask, *"Is that good news or bad news?"*

If Someone Misinterprets Your News

What to Say
- *"Actually, we look at Tony losing his job as an opportunity for some good changes for him and our family."*
- *"Unfortunately, we're not happy about the boy she is marrying. Will you keep us in your prayers?"*
- *"I'm sorry my mother is so sick, but our relationship was very difficult and it's kind of a relief that she is in the hospital where she's being cared for. Thank you for your thoughts."*
- *"I have mixed feelings . . . our son received a wonderful scholarship but the college is three states away!"*

What Not to Say
- *"I can't believe you thought that was good news when it was bad!"*
- *"I thought you knew me better than that!"*

What to Do
- If you are going to correct the person's misconception, do so immediately, and in a kind and polite way.

Don't ...
- ... be upset if someone misunderstands your news.
- ... let a significant misperception go uncorrected; the person will be embarrassed when he or she finds out your true feelings.
- ... correct the misperception unless you are willing to explain why the news is not as it seems. If the person is a good friend, you might want to go into details so you can talk about it further. If the person is an acquaintance you rarely see, or you're not comfortable sharing the details, you might decide not to correct the misperception.

Problems with Neighbors

If problems or misunderstandings occur between you and a neighbor, attempt to fix them as soon as possible.

What to Say
- *"You probably don't realize that your dog barks all day when you're gone, but it is disturbing us."*
- *"It was so windy the other day! I noticed garbage blowing from your cans; I don't know if you know that neighborhood rules say we have to keep our garbage contained so it doesn't blow into anyone's lawn."*
- *"We work really hard on our lawn, and I've noticed your kids riding their bikes across it. I'm sure they don't realize they're causing damage, but could you please ask them not to do that?"*

- *"We saw you riding your 4-wheeler across our property the other day—I hope you had a great time! However, we are growing a crop of hay out there, and riding on it damages the growing hay and causes ruts that can be dangerous when we harvest. We would appreciate it if you'd ride somewhere else."*
- *"I'm so glad your kids enjoy using our trampoline! However, it can be dangerous, so we need to make sure someone is here when they are doing so. Please make sure you are here, or your husband is, if they play on it again."*
- *"I noticed your dogs running through the neighborhood. Just this year, several dogs have been hit by cars and another was poisoned by fertilizer when he got into a neighbor's garage. I know how we all love our pets so just wanted to warn you; in this neighborhood, it's best to keep pets confined!"*

What Not to Say
- *"I can't believe you think it's OK to . . ."*
- *"You are very un-neighborly to . . ."*

What to Do
- Pray for God's guidance to act and speak kindly and appropriately.
- Before you talk with your neighbor, remember that in doing so you risk him reacting defensively or creating hard feelings between the two of you. Weigh the importance of the problem verses possibly making the problem worse by confronting your neighbor about the problem.
- If you do choose to talk with your neighbor, do so kindly; clearly state the problem and your proposed solution, and continue to be friendly with the neighbor if possible.
- Call the police or homeowner's association if appropriate.

Don't . . .
- . . . confront a neighbor who appears to be inebriated or violent.

Chapter 8

Encouraging Words

In our day-to-day lives, we often forget to encourage others. Our words—positive or negative—are very powerful. When you say something encouraging to someone, you are giving valuable support. Proverbs 16:24 says *"Pleasant words are as a honeycomb; sweet to the soul and healing to the bones."* Consider making it a personal challenge to offer someone sweet and healing words, every day.

When A Friend is Making a Big Decision

When a friend faces a big decision—a move, new job, going back to school—he will appreciate your support and encouragement.

What to Say
- *"I know you'll be fine no matter what decision you make."*
- Ask your friend leading questions to help guide his decision; *"How would doing that affect your goal to get your Master's Degree?" "Do you want to commute that far?" "How do you think it will affect your life 10 years from now?"*
- *"What are your options?"*
- *"Tell me what you've been thinking regarding this issue."*

What Not to Say
- *"Here's what you should do . . . "*
- *"If you do that, it would be a complete and total disaster!"*
- *"Well, that decision would sure be stupid!"* (Even if you think it would be, find a more tactful way to say it!)

What to Do
- Pray for your friend to be led to make the right decision.
- Encourage him as he works through the decision-making process.
- Be understanding if he seems nervous, short-tempered, or talks a lot about the decision he's facing.
- Try to help him break down the decision into small steps so he can see the different aspects of it, rather than the sometimes overwhelming whole.
- Offer to help (without influencing his decision) by proofreading his resume', helping him make a list of pros and cons about each side of the decision, listening to him talk through his thoughts and options.
- Remind him of his strengths.
- Support his decision.

Don't . . .
- . . . try to hurry or influence his decision; let him make it in his way, in his own time.
- . . . judge his decision.
- . . . make negative comments about his decision after he has made it.

Family Member Being Deployed

At this time in our country, family members are being deployed from many homes. Some families have several family members who will be, or are, deployed at the same time. Military personnel are being deployed several times, and sometimes deployments are extended. Family members will probably have mixed feelings about the deployment; pride in the bravery and accomplishments of the loved one who is in the military, and fear, anxiety, and sadness over the prospect of separation and their loved one(s) being in danger. When a loved one is, or his or her deployment is extended, family members need extra support.

What to Say
- *"How long will she be gone?"*
- *"We will certainly be praying for him."*
- *"How are you feeling about all of this? How are the kids?"*
- *"Our country is blessed to have men and women willing to serve our country like he is."*
- *"I'm so thankful that she is willing to serve."*
- *"May I write to him? What can I send her?"*

If someone is deployed again, or his return home is delayed;
- *"I'm so sorry he's leaving again/won't be home when you were planning!"*
- *"What a disappointment."*
- *"We will continue to pray for him, and for all of you."*
- *"It's OK to cry/be mad about the situation."*

What Not to Say
- *"Don't you know how dangerous it is over there? Aren't you totally freaked out about it?"*
- *"I can't believe the mess our country is in."*
- *"It's a mistake for our troops to be over there."* (Even if you feel this way, it's not appropriate to say it to someone whose loved one is being deployed.)

What to Do
- Pray for the safety and well-being of the person who is deployed, and for the well-being and peace of mind of the family members left behind.
- Ask about the person who is deployed, when you see family members.

- Remember that family members might not know, or might not be allowed to give, details of the mission or even where the person is stationed.
- Remain positive, but if the person you're talking to mentions the dangers, do not minimize his feelings; validate them with, *"Yes, it is scary to think of him being in a war zone. God is watching over him and he'll be in our prayers."*
- Send cards or e-mails of support to the family members left behind, and to the person who is deployed; include reassuring Bible verses like Ps. 91, Ps. 23, Phillip. 4:6-7, Ps. 94:19.
- Offer your support to families while their loved one is gone. Take meals, offer to watch the kids, scoop snow or perform or help with other household tasks.

Don't . . .
- . . . make any political statements, or say anything negative about the military, regardless of your views.

Disappointment After Working Hard for Something

When a friend or relative has worked hard for a promotion, new job, to get into college, or win an award, and it didn't work out, share her disappointment and show her your support.

What to Say
- *"Oh no! You worked so hard for that!"*
- *"I'm proud of you for trying."*
- *"You seem so disappointed—I would be too."*
- *"I'm sad for you . . . "*
- *"It's OK to be mad/sad/upset."*
- *"What's next?"* (This implies your acceptance of the person whether she decides to try again, start something new, or move in a different direction.)
- *"Everything happens for a reason,"* or, *"When one door closes, another opens."*

What Not to Say
- *"Oh well, I knew it wouldn't work from the start."*
- *"It was such a long shot—why did you even bother trying?"*
- *"That just shows it's not worth it to work so hard for something."*
- *"You should have known it wasn't meant to be."*

What to Do
- Call and ask your friend how she's doing.
- Remind your friend of her strengths.
- Encourage her to try again when another opportunity comes along.
- Send a thinking-of-you card; include passages like Rom. 8:28, Phillip. 1:6, and Eph. 2:10.

Don't . . .
- . . . gossip about the situation to others.
- . . . discourage her from trying again.

Compliments

Giving Compliments

As well as complimenting people on big accomplishments—a raise, promotion, publishing a book, successfully managing a volunteer event, pulling off a surprise party or coordinating a fun family event—notice and compliment people for everyday deeds and actions. Compliment people you don't know, too! Don't forget to praise your spouse and children; people often taken for granted. No matter who you compliment, you'll have the satisfaction of knowing you've added a bright spot to their day.

What to Say
- *"Good for you!"*
- *"All of your hard work and planning paid off—great job!"*
- *"You worked so hard for that—congratulations!"*
- *"What a fantastic accomplishment!"*

- *"We will all remember the fun of this day for a long time—thank you for all you did to make it happen."*
- To your spouse; *"Thank you for killing that spider! Since I'm petrified of bugs, I'm so grateful to have you to do that." "Thank you for working so hard for our family!" "You are such a good father; thank you for spending so much time with the kids."*
- To your child; *"It was so nice of you to help your brother when he dropped his books on the way to the bus this morning." "Thank you for straightening up the kitchen! It was so nice to walk in and see it clean—it really made my day."*
- To a teacher; *"I know teachers work very hard—I appreciate the long hours you work and the effort you put into making class interesting for my children."*
- To your hostess at Bible Study; *"What a beautiful home you have!"*
- To anyone at work or a get-together; *"That dress looks great on you; what a pretty color."*
- To your clergy person; *"Thank you for your hard work in arranging the special services."*
- To any mom; *"I admire how patient you are with your children."*
- To a tired-looking mom in the grocery store; *"Your kids are so cute, and well behaved! I can tell you're a great mom."*
- To any friend or acquaintance; *"You are always so cheerful and I look forward to seeing you. It brightens my day!"*
- To a stranger; *"You sang so beautifully at the concert! Singing is not one of my talents so I really admire anyone who can get up in front of people and do that."*
- To a co-worker; *"Great job with the presentation! You're always so calm under pressure."*
- *"Thank you for listening; I really needed someone and you were there."*
- *"Thanks for your e-mail—I really needed to hear that and appreciate your taking the time to write."*

What Not to Say
- *"Couldn't you have done _____ to make it better?"*
- *"I did that exact thing last year . . . "*
- *"You should have gotten that promotion last year."*
- Obviously false praise; *"I just loved your okra, beet, and tuna casserole!"* when you left most of it on your plate.
- *"That was absolutely the most fantastic, marvelous, beautiful rendition of that song that has ever been sung! You should get a recording contract and become a professional singer!"* Obviously, this praise is very overdone and likely to embarrass the person you are complimenting.

What to Do
- Praise the person in front of others; public acknowledgement gives the person an additional boost.
- Be cautious about praising people (especially children) on physical characteristics that they don't have control over, like long legs or pretty eyes. It is OK, however, to praise accomplishments when a person has been working on improving his or her body; *"I know you've been working out, and you look great!"*
- Put your praise in writing; the person will probably save your card or e-mail and feel your encouragement every time she reads it.

Don't . . .
- . . . give insincere praise; it is easy to detect.
- . . . overdo praise; you might be seen as being insincere, or having low standards.
- . . . automatically give a compliment back immediately after the person has complimented you; if you are searching for something to compliment, it will be obvious. (One example of an exception; if you're both dressed up for an event, it's OK to say, *"So do you!"* in reply to her, *"You look nice!"* as the compliment is obviously sincere.)

Accepting a Compliment

Many people are uncomfortable receiving a compliment, and their first response is to minimize what they're being complimented on. However, Proverbs 12:14 tells us that people will be rewarded for what they say. The person who compliments you is giving you a gift for which he, in turn, will be rewarded. If you minimize or contradict a compliment that is given to you, you are refusing a gift from the person who offered it.

Here are gracious replies to a compliment.

What to Say
- *"Thank you!"*
- *"Thanks! It makes my day to know I helped."*
- *"It was hard work, but definitely worth it."*
- *"Thank you—I hope you enjoy reading my book as much as I enjoyed writing it." "I enjoyed painting it for you and hope you'll enjoy it now, too." "Thank you—I had a lot of fun picking out this couch for our family."*
- *"Thank you—it's my favorite dress. I'm glad you like it too!"*

What Not to Say
- *"No I'm not!"* or anything that contradicts the person's compliment. No one wants to get into a contest about the compliment's validity.
- *"I didn't do much." "It was no big deal."* These replies imply the person shouldn't have given you the gift of a compliment.

What to Do
- Smile when you say, *"Thank you!"*
- E-mail the person to thank her for her compliment.
- Acknowledge others who played a part; *"I had a great team to work with." "My kids helped cook the supper; we're glad you enjoyed it!"*

Don't . . .
- . . . immediately come back with a compliment for the person who just complimented you; it may seem insincere.

Acknowledging a Difficult Decision

All of us struggle with difficult decisions—forgiving someone who has done wrong, whether or not to end a very difficult marriage, telling the truth despite the consequences, or doing the right thing no matter how difficult. Many times when faced with such a dilemma, people make a decision that has a negative impact on themselves and those around them. Acknowledging a difficult decision made the right way will encourage the person who made that decision.

What to Say
- *"I know you've been struggling with what to do; I'm so glad you made the decision you did."*
- *"Many people would have taken the easy way out. You did what was right. I admire you for doing that."*
- *"It takes a lot of courage to do what you did. I'm proud of you for doing so."*
- *"I know that was a difficult decision to make. You are a great example for other people faced with a similar situation."*

What Not to Say
- *"You should have . . ."*
- *"You sure did it the hard way!"*
- *"What took you so long to decide to do that?"*

What to Do
- Carefully consider whether to offer your praise privately or in public. It might be better to do it in private if few people knew of the dilemma, but if the problem was public knowledge, praising the person in public affirms his difficult decision and perhaps will encourage others to do the same.

Don't . . .
- . . . overdo your praise; this is probably a case for quiet satisfaction rather than outright celebration.

Acknowledgements

There were literally hundreds of people involved in the writing of this book and without each and every one of you, it would not have turned out as it did.

Thanks to the many, many people who talked to me in person, and contacted me via the internet, to tell me about their experiences and give me suggestions as to what to include in this book. Many shared painful events, and difficult times in their lives. All gave me valuable information that's included in this book. These "real life" experiences are what makes this book so useful and important.

Thanks to my husband Tim, who patiently put up with a messy house and thrown-together meals at times (many times?) while I was working on this book. Thanks to Cody and Morgan (our teenagers), who taught me things about how my computer works, that I would have never figured out on my own!

Thanks to my parents and grandparents who instilled in me the belief that I could accomplish anything I wanted to.

And thanks to God, Who guided me through this whole project, and sent friends, relatives, and strangers to encourage me when I needed a kind word the most.

Appendix

Asking the Holy Spirit to Guide Your Words

How do you comfort a friend during the darkest hours of his or her life? What do you say to someone who has received devastating news? At times we've all been confronted with a situation that is so unexpected, or awful, that knowing what to say is beyond our experience or knowledge, despite our desire to take away some of the pain of the person who is in crisis.

Do not think that you cannot help because you are too young, or too old, too inexperienced, or have not been in the same situation as the person who is suffering. God can and does use us to comfort others, sometimes when we feel the least qualified to do so.

Romans 8:26-27 tells us that, *". . . the Spirit helps us in our weakness. We do not know what we ought to pray for, but the Spirit Himself intercedes for us with groans that words cannot express. And He Who searches our hearts knows the mind of the Spirit, because the Spirit intercedes for the saints in accordance with God's will."* When you are faced with a situation and just do not know what words to say, take a deep breath and pray for the Holy Spirit to give you the words. You don't even have to have words to pray; He can interpret your 'groans,' or pleas, for the right words to come to you, through God and the Holy Spirit.

Then, wait . . . do not hurry to reply to what your friend has said, or fill a silence. Your quiet presence will be a comfort to your friend.

Listen for God's still, small voice, urging you what to say or do, and use those words to help or comfort your friend.

Proverbs 16:1 tells us, *"To man belong the plans of the heart, but from the Lord comes the reply of the tongue."* When the plans of our heart are to comfort someone, or talk with them about a serious situation, God knows this. If we seek Him, He will give us the right words to reply with.

The Bible is full of verses that show us the importance of our words. Ask God to guide your words and use them as He desires.

Tone of Voice
(Using Tone of Voice to Your Advantage)

Your tone of voice is as important as the words you say (or maybe more!) in getting your message across.

Many women raise pitch of their voices at the end of each sentence, making each sentence sound like a question. If you do this, you sound uncertain about what you are saying, and people may not take what you say seriously. Listen to yourself to see if you do this; if you do, concentrate on keeping your voice at the same pitch and making statements, not uncertain, unintended questions.

If your voice is very soft, and not firm, you may sound unsure of yourself and uncertain about the validity of what you are saying. A soft tone of voice may reflect your gentle and easygoing personality, but it may also send the signal that you're not sure about what you are saying, and during discussions your words can be easily drowned out by others. If this describes you, concentrate on making your voice a little louder, and much firmer (imagine your words traveling to a point across the room), when you speak.

If you are in a conversation that is getting intense—when you're trying to make a point or involved in an argument, for example—you'll probably tend to speak faster, and in a higher tone of voice. To regain control of your emotions, and the conversation, take a deep breath, collect your thoughts, slow down your speech, and speak in a slightly lower voice. These actions will help you to make your points more effectively.

If you want people to listen to you, lower your tone of voice, and take a deep breath before you speak, so your words sound solid and sincere. Speak slowly. Some people lower the volume of their voice, especially if people around them aren't paying attention; speaking more quietly—but still firmly—catches people's attention better than speaking loudly in some situations.

10 Worst Things to Say in Any Situation

Sometimes we're tempted to use these phrases because we're so uncomfortable with a grieving or suffering person's emotions. Resist the temptation and do not say them! Instead, use one of the phrases on the next page, which will be much more comforting and helpful.

"I know just EXACTLY how you feel!"

"Don't worry, it will all work out perfectly and everything will be just fine."

"Here's what you need to do . . . "

"It can't be THAT bad!"

"Get over it! You've felt that way long enough."

"You've grieved enough."

"You're not grieving in the 'right' way."

"Don't feel that way!"

"Don't say that!"

"Don't cry!"

10 Best Things to Say When You Don't Know What to Say

No matter what the situation or circumstance, one or more of these statements are the 'right' thing to say.

"I'm so sorry!"

"You are in my thoughts and prayers"

"What can I do for you?"

"It's OK to cry/scream/laugh."

"It's OK to be mad/sad/upset/confused."

"There are many people who love and support you"

"This is a terrible time for you, but I know you can do what you have to do."

"I am here any time you want to talk/e-mail/cry."

"I am your friend and I will support you and be here for you no matter what!"

NOTHING—just give a hug or sit quietly and listen.

Index

Abusive relationship,
   if a friend is in, ... 181

Addicted, if you suspect a
   friend is, ... 186

Adoption, ...69-71
   if plans fall through, ...70-71
   when friends adopt, ...69-70
   when you adopt, ...70-71

Advice 21-26
   asking for, ... 24
   giving, ...21-22
   when you are given, ... 25

Anniversary
   after death of a
      loved one, ...148-151
   after divorce, ... 59
   of miscarriage, ... 146

Baby
   born with special needs
      or a disability, ...171-173
   death of, ...147-151
   significant dates after, ...148-151

Beliefs
   personal, and lifestyle
      choices, ...33-34
   other people's, respecting, ... 34

   yours, expressing, ... 33
   political, ... 36
   religious, ... 36

Best things to say in any
   situation, ... 220

Bigoted remarks or jokes, ...50-51

Child/children
   behaving badly 77-80
   someone else's child(ren), ...77-79
   your children, ... 80
   chronic illness, ...167-169
   death of, ...147-151
   significant dates after, ...149-151
   disability or special needs,
      with, ...174-175
   environment of other
      children's homes, if you're
      not comfortable with, ...75-76
   other children not getting
      along with your child, ...72-74
   rules of your home, other
      children not following, ...74-75

Comments, inappropriate, rude,
   critical, obnoxious, ... 81

Compliments
   accepting, ... 212
   giving 209-212

Dates, significant
   after death of a loved one,... 148-152
   after death of a child, ... 149
   after divorce, ... 59-60
   after miscarriage, ... 146

Death, providing comfort to
   loved ones, ... 119-153
   anniversaries after a
     death 149, 151
   between the death and the
     funeral 123
   funeral, at 125
   holidays, ... 149, 151
   immediately after, ... 119-123
   long-term—weeks and
     months after, ... 126-132
   of a pet, ... 152-153
   significant dates, after 148, 151

Decisions, difficult
   acknowledging, ... 213
   when someone is making,... 205-206

Deployment, when family
   member facing, ... 206-208

Depression, when a friend is
   experiencing, ... 184

Disappointment after working
   hard for something, ... 208-209

Dying
   loved ones of person
     who is, ... 137-138
   person who is, ... 134-137

Family
   dysfunctional, general
     guidelines for dealing
     with, ... 101-102
   friend's, when having
     difficulties, ... 111-113

   when cut ties with or limit
     contact with, 113-115
   when member needs more
     care, ... 115-116
   when member in
     long-term-care, ... 116-117
   member being deployed, ... 206-208
   sexual advances or
     comments, ... 110-111
   spouse's, ... 111
   yours
     embarrassing family
       member, ... 109-110
     limiting contact with, ... 105-106
     explaining to other family
       members, ... 107-109
     visits, where to stay, ... 103-104

Favors, ... 26-33
   accepting, ... 31
   asking for, ... 29
   offering, ... 26
   saying "no" to a request for, ... 27
   turning down when offered, ... 31

Fertility, problems with, ... 61-68
comebacks to thoughtless
   questions about, ... 63
pregnancy or baby shower,
   announcing, ... 64-66
pregnancy or baby shower,
   responding to if you are
     having problems, ... 67-68
when someone else is having
   problems, ... 61-64
when you are having
   problems, ... 66-68

Foot-in-mouth, when you put
   your, ... 199

Gossip, ... 40-43

Holidays
    celebrating after the death
        of a loved one, ... 148-153
    celebrating after divorce, ... 59-60

Holy Spirit, asking Him to guide
    your words 217-218

Illness and Injury.................... 155-176
    acute, person with
        injury/illness, ... 155-164
    recovery, lengthy, ... 161-164
    spouse/caregiver, ... 157, 162
    chronic................................ 164-167
    child with, ... 167
    ongoing, ... 166
    when diagnosed, ... 164

Invitation, if someone
    asks for 195-197

Job
    reference, someone asks
        you for, ... 180
    someone losing theirs, ... 43
    you losing yours, ... 44

Jokes, sexist, racist, bigoted, ... 50

Marriage
    expressing concerns about
        someone's upcoming, ... 53-56
    problems and divorce, yours
        and someone else's, ... 56-61
    holidays and anniversaries
        during and after 59-60

Miscarriage, ... 144-146
    anniversary of due date, ... 148

Money problems, ... 45-49
    someone else's, ... 45-48
    yours, ... 48-49

Neighbors, problems with, ... 203

News
    when you don't know if it's
        good or bad, ... 201-202
    when your news is
        misinterpreted, ... 202-203

People/personalities, difficult
    attitude, person with
        "poor me," 88-90
    crisis, person who constantly
        experiences, ... 91-93
    critical, person who is, ... 87-88
    cursing in public, ... 90-91
    drama king or queen, ... 84-86
    negative, person who is, ... 86-87
    responsibility, person who
        won't take, ... 93-95
    talks too much, person
        who, ... 83-84

Politics, discussing, ... 36-39

Pregnancy
    someone else's, when you're
        having fertility problems, ... 67-68
    unexpected
        unmarried child of
            friend, ... 188-190
        friend, ... 190-191
    yours, announcing when
        someone else is having
        fertility problems, ... 64-66

Questions, inappropriate, rude,
    critical, obnoxious, ... 81

Racist remarks or jokes, ... 50-51

Religion, discussing, ... 36-39

Secrets 191-195
    friend sharing, ... 193-195

yours, sharing,....................191-193

Sexist remarks or jokes,...............50-51

Sexual assault, friend has
 been victim of,..........................183

Shy, getting through events
 when you are,..............................51

Spouse
 bashing,.......................................49
 family members of,...................111
 potential, expressing your
  concerns about,........................53

Suicide
 if friend has attempted,......187-188
 when someone dies by,......142-144
 when someone threatens,...138-142

Voice, tone of, using to your
 advantage,..........................218-218

Worst things to say in any
 situation,....................................219

Printed in the United States
200017BV00003B/271-285/A